Dedication

For the unfettered barefoot freedom they gave me to roam the wilds as a small boy, I thank my parents Gwen & Bert Elliott and my maternal grandparents Anne & David Black and I dedicate this book to them.

Alan Elliott

The *Presidential*

Elephants *of Zimbabwe*

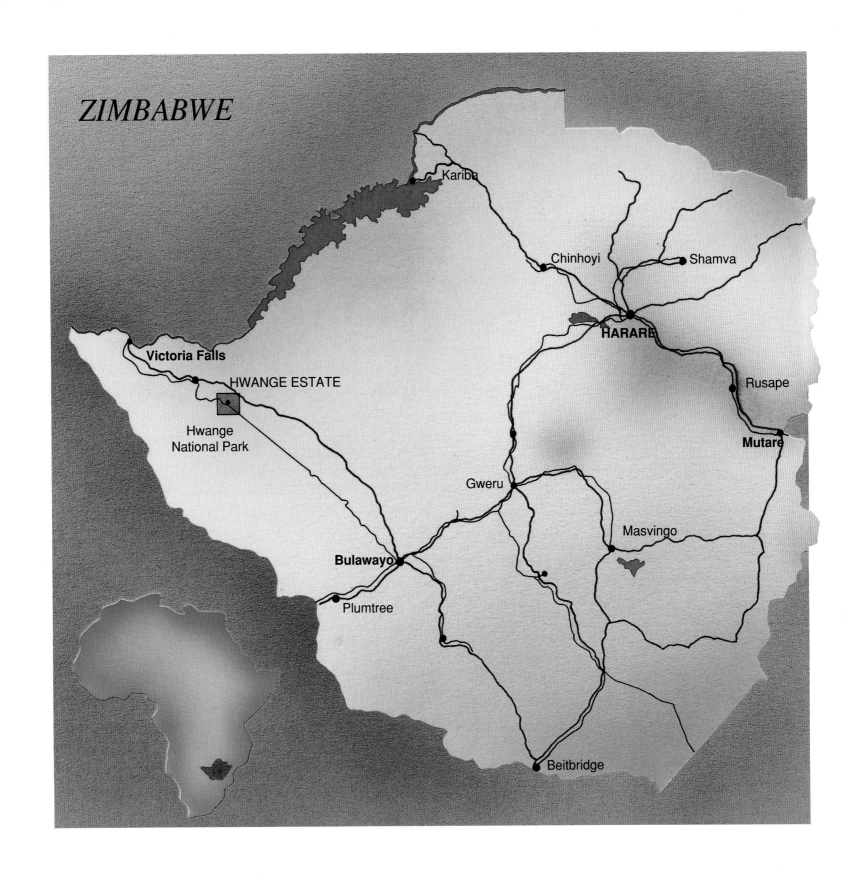

ZIMBABWE

Kariba

Chinhoyi · Shamva

Victoria Falls HARARE

HWANGE ESTATE Rusape

Hwange
National Park Mutare

Gweru

Masvingo

Bulawayo

Plumtree

Beitbridge

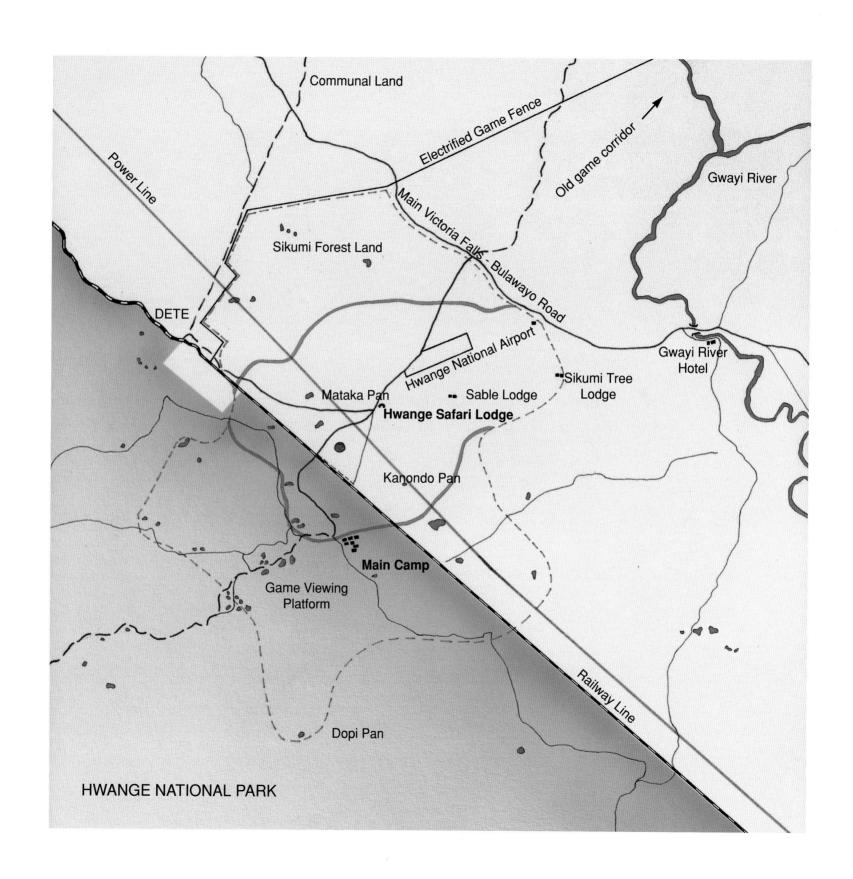

Communal Land

Electrified Game Fence

Old game corridor

Power Line

Gwayi River

Sikumi Forest Land

Main Victoria Falls - Bulawayo Road

DETE

Hwange National Airport

Gwayi River Hotel

Mataka Pan

Sable Lodge

Sikumi Tree Lodge

Hwange Safari Lodge

Kanondo Pan

Main Camp

Game Viewing Platform

Railway Line

Dopi Pan

HWANGE NATIONAL PARK

Alan Elliott

The Presidential Elephants of Zimbabwe

ISBN No. 0 - 7974 - 1003 - 1

Copyright Delta Operations Pvt Ltd 1991
PO Box 294, Borrowdale, Harare, Zimbabwe

Produced by The Corporate Brochure Company
36 Finborough Road, London SW10 9EG

Designed by Pilcher Graphics Ltd., PO Box 30806, Lusaka, Zambia

Typeset by Superskill Graphics Pte Ltd, 79 Indus Road, Singapore

Colour separations, printing and binding by Craft Print Pte Ltd, 9 Joo Koon Circle, Singapore 2262.

Illustration and Photography

David Shepherd OBE FRSA painting on page 115 and drawings on pages 68 and 69.

The photographs are by:

David Paynter: *10,17,20,26,31,33,40,41,50,51,55,58,59,60,64,65,74,79a,85,86,91,104,106,108,109,111,117,126,127, 128,129,130,132,139.*

Jan and Fiona Teede: *12,16,19,28,29c,35,39,57,72,73,76,77,79b,81,82,83,90,99,112a,123b.*

Guy Hobbs: *21,29a,30,32a,32b,32c,34,38,66,71,75,78b,93a,100a,100b,101,102,110,113,116,120b,122,136,140,143.*

Alan Elliott: *2,3,18,21,22,24,29b,36,37,53,63,70,78a,88,89,92,93,95b,119,120a,123a,124,125.*

National Archives: *42,43,44,45,47,48,49.*

Ian Murphy: *25,60,75,133.*

Greg Elliot: *13.*

Illustration by:

David Boys: *120,134,135.*

Foreword

Conservation is about the long term survival of Man himself. It has gained increasing prominence throughout the world in recent years and the plight of many threatened species, including that of the African Elephant, has been brought sharply into focus.

The international community is being forced to appreciate that the pressing needs of human beings on this planet can no longer be viewed in isolation. Human population growth has accelerated at an unprecedented pace and, more than ever before, governments everywhere are faced with the problem of having to balance the conflicting needs of man and the environment.

Economic difficulties and the demands of fashion have spawned a massive poaching 'industry'. The lucrative illegal trade in commodities such as elephant ivory and rhino horn has led to a catastrophic decline in these large mammals on much of the African continent, where over 60% of the elephant population is believed to have been slaughtered in the last decade alone. Zimbabwe, however, has a sound scientific and technical wildlife management infrastructure, supported by forward-thinking legislation. A cornerstone objective of our wildlife management policy is to attempt to maintain the ecological balance between our plant communities, their dependent animal populations and the needs of the human community. This has sometimes necessitated the scientific control of elephant numbers in certain areas and the sale of by-products such as ivory. Our particular circumstances have not always been fully understood by the international conservation movement.

Whilst acutely aware that much remains to be done, (and learned) we can be proud of the Zimbabwe Government's record in the conservation of our natural resources. I must also pay tribute to the valuable contribution made both by dedicated public officials as well as many private individuals. This commitment is typified by the imaginative approach of Alan Elliott and all those who, over the years, have worked in harmony to foster the unique Presidential Elephants of Zimbabwe.

It is my hope that the Presidential herd, under my patronage, will be seen as a symbol of my personal commitment and that of all Zimbabweans to conservation. I would also like to see it stimulate further international research on these magnificent animals and their relationship with a world we all have to share.

COMRADE ROBERT GABRIEL MUGABE

His Excellency, The President of the Republic of Zimbabwe

Acknowledgements

The idea for this book came from Alun Thomas and the inspiration from Ron Stringfellow. David Paynter's enthusiasm and ideas got the project moving. An approach first to Pat Rooney and then to Enos Chiura for financial backing from Delta Corporation met with an immediate and positive response. Alistair Wright of Zimbabwe Sun Hotels has always been most supportive.

Mrs Amina Hughes, the Deputy Minister of Transport did not know what she was letting herself in for when she agreed to get involved on behalf of her beloved elephants. I cannot sufficiently thank Mrs Hughes and Comrade Didymus Mutasa, Senior Minister for Political Affairs for putting the case for Presidential Status of the elephants before His Excellency, President Mugabe, and for all their work in bringing this dream to fruition.

My thanks go to Pip Maxwell, Bruce Campbell and Kim Kraan in the Harare office for hours and hours of administrative work. In addition to our principal photographers, I would like to thank Greg Elliot and John Burton for offering supporting material and especially to Ian Murphy.

David Shepherd OBE FRSA, a true and generous friend of African wildlife generously donated his especially produced and magnificent illustrations. Thanks also to David Boys for last minute artistic assistance willingly rendered, Les McClaggen for sorting out the original typing and introducing me to floppy discs and to Cannias Mwatsia of the National Archives.

We were fortunate to have the outstanding photographic skills of David Paynter, Jan and Fiona Teede and Guy Hobbs, whose work has its own eloquence.

Thanks to Gerry Davison and Garry Haines in Hwange for background information. In Singapore Ian Murphy, George Metcalfe, and Mick Pilcher of CBC worked round the clock. Charlie and Dora Chan and Roger Phua of Craft Print pulled out all the stops to have the book ready on time. In particular I wish to express my deepest gratitude to my editor, George Metcalfe for his sagacity and to Lillian, his wife for their kindness and hospitality. John and Pat Arscot have put up with me in Australia and taught me to type with two fingers. My wife, Scotty, has supported my dreams for many years, and I am grateful to her for living with me in pretty difficult conditions in a variety of tents, tree houses, and huts.

In order to set the record straight, and lest I give the impression that I have been solely responsible for the development of the Hwange Estate and the acclimatisation of the Presidential Elephants, I wish to acknowledge the role of all our staff who have worked with the elephants. It has taken a combined and disciplined approach by everyone, which has led to an acceptance by the elephants. To all our rangers, past and present, I wish to acknowledge your role and in particular the key role of Garth Thompson.

Preface

This book is in no way to be considered a weighty scientific tome. I was lucky enough to grow up in the Zimbabwe bush and this, rather than the library has been my classroom. With others, I have been greatly privileged to have been entrusted with the care of the Elephants of the Hwange Estate on the edge of the great Hwange National Park in Zimbabwe. I have studied the herd as it has grown from a small group of 22 petrified elephants in the early 1970s to a robust, confident population of over 300 animals today.

In essence, this is a very personal account about gaining the trust of the Hwange Estate elephants, many of whom I have come to know well. It is also about the environment in which they live. Over a period of twenty years my colleagues and I working in photographic safaris have helped to introduce our elephants and other wildlife at Hwange to tens of thousands of visitors from all parts of the world. Hopefully we have succeeded in communicating our affection and enthusiasm for these four-legged Zimbabwean ambassadors. Perhaps too, our guests have taken back to their own countries happy memories of their encounters with elephants and a positive impression of the fine work being undertaken by both government and the private sector on behalf of wildlife in Zimbabwe.

Never before has the Head of State of any country bestowed personal patronage on a specific herd of elephants, and I am particularly grateful to His Excellency, the President of Zimbabwe, Comrade Robert Mugabe, for placing this world famous herd under his protection. Henceforth they are to be known as 'The Presidential Elephants of Zimbabwe'.

It is widely accepted that elephants have a great capacity to modify the habitat in which they live. My own views on what is an acceptable density of elephants on the Kalahari sandveldt are sometimes at variance with current official opinion. The arguments about elephant population reduction are by no means conclusive and will always be debated. This is why ongoing research is absolutely vital.

Now that our elephants have been given special Presidential Status we are committed to a long term research programme in a quest to understand more about these animals and the environment in which they live. This is the 100,000 acre Hwange Estate. It was conceived by a number of forward-thinking pioneers, chief of whom were John Carter of Delta Corporation and Mike Routledge, who, with the late Johnny Uys, brought this unique wildlife sanctuary into being from a patchwork of land held under various titles. In the past it had been little more than a killing ground for 19th century ivory hunters, rich 'sportsmen', and latterly, as a nursery shooting range for all and sundry.

Today the roar of the muzzle loader and rifle have been replaced by the more peaceful sound of the camera shutter in this idyllic wildlife setting. The elephants give untold pleasure to visitors who come bent not on killing the largest tusker for its ivory, but rather to learn and to capture for ever its *living* images.

After reading this book I hope you will agree with me that the African Elephant is worthy of our love, care and respect.

Alan Elliott
Sikumi Tree Lodge, Hwange Estate

The Crop Raiders

Early in 1974 the railway village of Dete on the eastern boundary of Zimbabwe's great Hwange National Park was a thriving community of some 600 people living in comfortable houses in a low density suburb of the village. It was typical of most railway communities hard drinking, fun loving, here today, gone tomorrow people. Nearby was a high density, low cost housing settlement into which were packed thousands of lower paid African workers with their families.

In order to augment their meagre incomes, most of these families cultivated small plots of maize, millet and melons on a large tract of land between the protected Sikumi Forest Area and their own housing units. The social centre of this community was the beer garden, where nightly many hundreds of patrons would assemble to enjoy the locally brewed African beer. As the alcohol took its effect, the noise from the beer garden could be heard up to two miles away. Towards midnight, as the patrons staggered to their various homes and fell asleep, quiet would descend on the village, broken only by the occasional barking of dogs.

In the still of an overcast February night, a herd of elephants was clustered along the boundary dividing the maize fields and the Sukumi Forest area. The forest area was part of the newly proclaimed Hwange Estate, set up for the purpose of conserving wildlife with a view to developing tourism. As the cow elephants quietly assembled in the forest near the maize fields, a few bulls had already stepped over the low, three stranded barbed wire fence. Slowly and carefully, with trunks up, all senses alert, they began to make their way towards the maize fields, the seductive smell of the crops enticing them forward.

As the herd of young cows nervously waited, one of them with half an ear missing put out her trunk to a sister, one of whose tusks had grown back towards her chest. The largest cow of all was tuskless whilst one of her relatives had only one tusk.

This group of cows could have been recognised anywhere by their individual physical abnormalities. Clustered round in quiet obedience were some small calves and younger females and a few sub-pubertal bulls ranging between four to twelve years of age. In all, the party numbered 14 animals.

As they moved steadily forward into the maize field, with the breeze behind them, the bulls could detect no human scent to suggest the presence of the enemy. What scent there was suggested that it was some hours old and therefore represented no danger. The bull elephants reached the field and started feeding. The cow herd, once assured, now entered into the maize field over the flattened barbed wire fence.

Waiting silently in ambush in a Landrover nearby, two game rangers from the adjoining Hwange National Park were alerted by the rustle of maize stalks. In whispered tones, the order to move in for the kill was given. Two marksmen, each with a heavy calibre rifle and followed by two teams carrying 12 volt car batteries connected to spotlights, carefully made their way through the three metre high stalks towards the sound of the feeding elephants.

At some 40 yards from the sound of feeding, the rangers split up and moved forward about 15 paces apart. The one on the right tensely awaited the indications that the elephants were close enough for his light to be switched on, and for the shooting to commence. From his position in the dark he estimated that there were about six or eight elephants around him. Suddenly, to his left, the other bright spotlight was switched on. A second or two later a loud report from a .458 rifle reverberated through the African night.

Wild panic from the unsuspecting elephants ensued. Immediately shouting to his attendant game scouts to turn on his own spotlight, the young ranger made ready to fire. In the confusion and haste, one of the battery clips was pulled off so that further lighting of the scene was impossible.

Stranded in the dark and petrified of being trampled, the ranger

loaded his rifle and braced himself. The crashing of maize stalks, the sound of running feet and the screaming of elephants created a frightening atmosphere. The thought passed through his mind that he had volunteered for this assignment. He now began to regret that he had ever done so and became convinced that he and his two game scouts would be crushed to death in the darkness. Fortunately no one was trampled in the stampede as the elephants fled headlong in panic towards the security of the Sukumi Forest, flattening the maize stalks ahead of them as they ran.

The very worst fears of the cow herd had been realised. In the instant that the shot was fired, they, too, had turned and fled, carefully protecting their offspring between them as they ran in wild alarm, snapping the wire fence at the boundary of the fields.

One of the bulls had been mortally wounded. Instinctively, he followed in the wake of the herd, only to fall a short distance away with blood choking his lungs. Death followed soon afterwards. The cow herd continued their flight for many miles until they reached the safety offered by the thick bush scrub near where a new hotel had been constructed. It was only then, within the depths of this tangled 'sinanga', that they stopped and re-grouped, raising their trunks to search for the tell-tale stench of their human pursuers.

For several days the elephants did not leave their thick bush sanctuary. It was only after two days and in the dead of night that they ventured forth for their first drink of water. It took several more days for the trauma of that February night to wear off, and once again, firmly etched in the minds of that elephant herd another incident confirmed the aggressive invincibility of that most feared of all adversaries, man.

Over the years, members of this family of elephants and other relatives of their group had been subjected to attacks both at night and during the day, and constant vigilance was always required. A lapse could have meant the death of one or more members of the group at any time. It was therefore always necessary to drill into the calves all the age-old precautions that had been passed down from generation to generation on the avoidance of conflict with man and to instil the deepest fear and respect for this super-predator which, unlike other predators, would often kill for the simple joy of killing.

On the Hwange Estate in 1990 a Landrover was parked at a waterhole called Kanondo near that same sinanga thicket. Standing in the Landrover, was a man, part of that race of hated predators. An elephant who had been collecting mineral salts in a nearby mineral lick strode purposefully towards him, put out his trunk and caressed the outstretched hand of the man in the vehicle. The elephant, now a bull in his early twenties, had been a young calf in that raiding party in the maize fields of Dete village on that fateful February night of 1974. Ndebele is the name of the elephant bull. I was the man in the Landrover. Much had happened in the intervening 16 years.

Such contact
between man and
free-roaming
elephants is rarely
seen.

An Ancient Land

The Hwange area in remote north western Zimbabwe was at one time a vast wilderness and, because of limited water supplies and the presence of mosquitoes and tsetse flies, a hostile environment for man. Because it was so large and virtually uninhabited it was selected in 1928 as Southern Rhodesia's (now Zimbabwe's) first national park. On the southern boundary of the 140 square km Hwange Estate, which is commonly shared with Hwange National Park (an area of 14,000 square km), is the Bulawayo/Victoria Falls railway line. Built in 1904, it was part of the Cape to Cairo railway dream of the colonial empire-builder, Cecil Rhodes.

Within this rectangular-shaped locality is an ancient forest region through which runs the beautiful and ecologically significant Dete Vlei (valley).

If we start our journey in the east and move westwards from the railway line, we enter a belt of Terminalia, or Mangwe trees. A kilometre away is the open calcrete area of Kanondo. Calcrete is predominantly limestone which is in the process of changing into rock.

This is where we are more likely to encounter elephants than anywhere else in the whole Hwange region. Everything the animals need is here - water, an abundant variety of food and mineral salts as well as mud for wallowing. After 20 years, they know they will not be molested by man.

The presence of potassium, sodium, calcium and other essential trace elements in the calcrete is vital because the surrounding area, blanketed as it was by Kalahari sand, is deficient in these minerals which are necessary to maintain health. Many other animals such as kudu, sable antelope, zebra, impala, the rare roan antelope, buffalo, giraffe and their predators - lions, leopards and Cape hunting dogs - also frequent Kanondo.

In this open area you can see large excavations, often with three or four elephants in them, almost hidden from view.

People often refer to these places as 'salt licks', but 'mineral licks' are more correct. The elephants themselves chisel out large quantities of mineralised earth with their tusks which they transfer to their mouths with their trunks. When the elephants are not there, the kudu and other animals take their turn at licking the soil.

These excavations become very large and form the basis of new pans (or ponds). The rain falls, the sides collapse, the elephants wallow and 'puddle' the mud, increasing its impermeability. The Kanondo Pan has been formed over centuries in this way and is continually being enlarged. This is just one of many examples of habitat modification by the elephant for the benefit of itself and other animals.

Moving away from Kanondo, you are soon enveloped in the most beautiful, natural Kalahari woodland forest in the whole region. Massive Camel Thorn trees *(Acacia erioloba),* giant Umtshibis *(Guiobortia coleosperma)* and Zimbabwe teak *(Baikiaea plurijuga)* trees spread their branches, offering welcome shade in the hottest months. This is a busy forest.

An elephant mother teaches her calf how to excavate for minerals

Clean water at Kanondo Pan is pumped into a trough near the acacia tree in the middle distance. With its mineral salts, mud and assured safety, Kanondo is greatly favoured by the elephants.

Animals of all descriptions are constantly moving back and forth from the Kanondo waterhole. There are a mass of tracks imprinted into the sand. Nutrients in the form of dung and decomposing vegetation are constantly being cycled into the soil by constantly passing hooves and feet.

You can walk through this for several miles before eventually dropping down into the wide, open, grassy valley of the Dete vlei.

Continuing the journey in a north eastward direction, you walk up a hundred metre wooded sand dune, covered with Terminalia and the very stately Red Syringa (*Burkea africana*) trees. Once up on the crest of the ridge you pass through teak and umtshibi woodland again, encountering beautiful Brachystegia country which carries through to the Victoria Falls road, interspersed here and there with such eye-catching large trees known as the Scotsman's Rattle and the baobab-like Mugongo trees commonly called Zimbabwe balsa. Further on, the area is bisected by a few minor valleys which have been invaded by woody scrub as a result of the drying out of the habitat. The chief of these valleys is the Zingweni.

It is a constant source of wonderment to me that this woodland habitat of sand and low rainfall offers a changing beauty all the year round. In the coldest winter months of June and July, when night time temperatures often sink below freezing, the dominant Zimbabwe teak trees become a magnificent show of gold, orange, yellow and brown, redolent of the splendour of the Fall of the north eastern United States.

At this time of the year most of the deciduous trees shed their leaves. In early August, a stark greyness overtakes the land. Then early one morning the arrival of our summer is

The lush Dete vlei in summer, where zebra find excellent grazing

Right: This elephant is in complete harmony with his environment, a typical example of the resilient Kalahari sand woodland.

Weather builds up during the hot, dry months at the Hwange National Park.

announced by the sound of bees overhead. One looks up to see the canary yellow flowers and green leaves of the *Acacia erioloba* once more bursting into life. Every year I am always taken by surprise at this sudden transformation. Within a day or two the small, dark green leaves of these majestic trees develop in profusion and provide a shady umbrella. At this time of the year you can always find elephants and other game under the acacias since they provide the only shade in this sun-baked landscape.

The giant acacias are also one of the favourite nesting sites of the Tawny Eagle. In August and September one can see both parents busily attending their solitary progeny at the nest. The timing of the nesting of the tawny eagle is crucial because, as you can imagine, trying to incubate an egg in a tree that is being constantly shaken for its pods by the elephants could be a no win situation! However, with the infinite timing of nature, there is no overlap in the activities of the pod-seeking elephants or the nesting tawny eagles.

The sprouting of the *acacia erioloba* trees and the sight of the newly born Eland calves is a signal that the harsh months of winter are past. The weather now warms up rapidly. Rainfall is at least two months away but the rapid increase in temperature stimulates the trees to draw on their root reserves of nutrients and moisture. It is another example of Nature's impeccable timing. Eland cows produce their calves exactly to coincide with the spring flush of new leaves upon which these browsing animals feed.

Unlike elephants, which have a broad breeding season in which young are predominantly born between the rainy months of November to March, the timing of the reproduction cycle of some other animals is critical. Warthogs, for instance, like all mammals, rely on an increased nutritional supply for the production of milk. They must give birth at a time of increased nutritional and protein levels in their food, but must not delay

until the advent of the rainy season. Virtually all the warthogs on Hwange Estate are born in the last two weeks in September. Their young are born without hair and need to remain in their underground burrows, where litter mates supply warmth to each other until they are robust enough to emerge at about four weeks. A flash flood would drown the young piglets. This is why birth must take place after the weather has warmed up, but before the onset of the rains.

Similarly, plovers, being ground nesting birds, must lay and hatch their eggs precisely before the rains. The onset of rain then ensures the emergence of an adequate supply of edible insects.

Apart from the new spring leaf which spreads gradually, the countryside maintains its stark character. The end of the harsh, dry, hot months is heralded in late October by the distant flashes of sheet lightening on the horizon. Gradually the intensity of the day and night time heat reaches such a build up that it feels impossible to continue existence without life-saving rain to cool off the earth. In fact in Zimbabwe we call this the "suicide month".

Within days dust storms gather momentum and whip across the landscape bringing swirling black clouds, often yielding no rain, as if in mockery of the suffering animal (and human) inhabitants of the bush. In most years this is soon followed by a build up of cumulus nimbus clouds and violent lightening storms. Tantalisingly, these often yield only a few large drops spattering the dry, parched earth, but leaving a most delicious smell, whose fresh, earthy sharpness can be only fully appreciated by those who have experienced it. When the rains finally arrive they are usually accompanied by a violent percussion of loud rolling thunder, the dark sky illuminated by piercing flashes of light as the fork lightning strikes the ground.

This is a hazardous time for animals. I recall vividly one morning waking up after a dry lightening storm to look out

from my house and to see under a lone umtshibi tree the carcasses of five dead wildebeeste strewn out at a distance of thirty or forty paces, their eyes blown out by the force of the lightening. On another occasion, after a similar storm, I saw two zebras lying dead in the Dete vlei, obviously struck by lightening. Turning one over to inspect it I found a flattened Crowned Plover, which had vainly attempted to shelter from the elements down wind of the zebra. I suspect the bird was killed by the falling zebra rather than the lightening!

Strangely I have never come across, or heard, of an elephant being killed by lightning.

By December, with the rainy season well-established, the *Ochna pulchra* trees are ablaze with yellow flowers and the Brachystegia (or Msasa) woodland takes on a shiny iridescence with its leaves erupting in a rainbow of colours, from lime green through to pinks, oranges and reds. After a few weeks of splendour, this new foliage reverts to its uniform green.

The main rains in Zimbabwe take place within what is known locally as the Intertropical Convergence Zone. A band of heavily laden moist air moves south from the equatorial belt in the north and converges with pressure systems from the south to cause precipitation. The Zimbabwe teak trees now come into flower, with their showy purple bouquets usually lasting for two to three months.

February in Hwange is the month of the heaviest rainfall and the Kalahari woodland assumes a cloak of green thicket impenetrability, where many varieties of flowers and shrubs display their colours.

In the Dete vlei, after particularly heavy rains, water lilies burst forth from the pans in a brilliant array of pointed blue petals. Some years when it is too dry they do not appear at all, but the miracle is that the edible lily bulb is always there ready to emerge from its mud bed when the conditions are right.

From year to year, nature triggers the appearance of various

Zebra, whose stripes are unique like fingerprints, are reflected in water of the rainy season along the Dete vlei.

Below: The teak trees bloom from December to February.

flowers which bloom on the shoulders of the valley as yellows or blues, or sometimes the reds of the wild Gladiolae.

This is the time when most of the young antelope and zebra can be seen frolicking in the early mornings across the luscious green carpet of the Dete vlei, giving vent to their expressions of joie de vivre. In particular the young impala race around playing and prancing with their characteristic rocking-horse motion, subconsciously honing defensive manoeuvres against future predators.

The grazing is at its peak on the grassy Dete vlei during the rainy season months of January and February. In contrast to the dry months when searching for nourishment is a constant activity, food is now so abundant for the sable antelope and other grazers like buffalo, tsessebe and wildebeeste that you can observe them at midday lying quietly and ruminating, their glossy coats shining in the sun.

Some evenings you can see young jackals, adolescent hyenas, families of crepuscular bush pigs, and some of the shyer mammals such as the spotted Serval cat, perched on

their vantage points along the vlei.

As you walk through the veldt tracking elephants, you come across many different examples of the type of vegetation they eat. One of the most interesting is the Mukwa or Blood Wood tree *(Pterocarpus angolensis)*. When the outer bark is stripped off, this tree gives off a red substance that resembles blood. It tastes rather like alum and is useful for the treatment of such ailments in man as gum sores or mouth ulcers. Some African people use a mixture of Mukwa sap in water for the treatment of diarrhoea. From my observations of the way in which the elephants utilise only small amounts of the bark it is possible that they too use it for medicinal rather than nutritional purposes.

Another observation I have made is the use by elephants of the tree Strychnos pungens. This tree is consumed almost exclusively during the hot month of September when it is drawing heavily on its root reserves. The tree contains quantities of strychnine, a well known poison. Strychnine is fed in small quantities by European pig farmers to their stock as a tonic. It is also used as a homeopathic medicine.

My hypothesis is that at this time of the year the elephants benefit in some way by the intake of small quantities of this alkaloid. Significantly, they do not appear to touch the plant at any other time of the year.

Clearly further research is required. By observing these remarkable animals more closely we may be able to increase our knowledge about other plants and their characteristics potentially beneficial to man.

Elephants also strip the bark from the Acacia erioloba trees and consume it. This is achieved by using their tusks to chisel at the outer bark and then, with the trunk, to pull off strips of the bark which is eaten. The bark of the Acacia erioloba contains about 9% calcium. In an area as impoverished as the Kalahari sandveldt it is clearly an important source of

Elephants select their food from a wide variety of plants according to seasonal availability. It is highly beneficial for seeds to pass through their digestive system.

this mineral. In the process, inevitably, a number of Acacias are killed by 'ring barking'. Whilst blame is put on the elephant for destruction of this tree it must also be borne in mind that elephants are also essential agents for the germination and redistribution of Acacia seeds.

I conducted an experiment in which I collected 100 seeds from fresh elephant dung and 100 from dry ripe pods. Under identical conditions 79 of the excreted seeds germinated against only 14 of the seeds from the pods.

I was not surprised with the result. The excreted seeds had already begun the process of germination within the animal's gut.

The outer husk had already been subjected to the animal's powerful digestive juices and the seed had already begun to swell under the conditions of heat and moisture in the dung. Significantly, after years of observation, elephants appear hardly to chew the acacia pods but swallow them whole. Presumably the digestive juices dissolve the outer husk leaving the pea-sized seed to pass through the digestive tract undamaged. It is thus greatly beneficial for the regeneration of acacias for their seeds to pass through the digestive tract of an elephant.

In spite of what is commonly believed, many species of trees are hardly touched by elephants, for example the Zimbabwe teak tree *(Baikiaea plurijuga)*, and the Umtshibi tree *(Guiobortia coleosperma)*. This is most fortuitous as these important hard woods are also a good source of shade for the animals.

In seasons of drought, when crops have failed, the African people from the nearby communal areas will enter the Hwange Estate to collect the husks from the seeds of the Umtshibi tree. These seeds, about the size of a small fingernail, are covered by a bright red shell. It is a painfully slow process to collect a bucketful, but the rewards are great as this is a high protein food. In the animal world, baboons particularly, like to collect and eat the husks.

The branches and bark of a beautiful little bush commonly

called the Violet tree *(Securidaca longepedunculata)* is favoured by the elephants as a food source. When I am out tracking and find this bush, I will often dig out a root and invite my guests to smell it. Lightly scraped, it gives off a pleasantly strong smell of wintergreen.

Elephants are very fond of Mugongo nuts. They come from *Rhycinodendron rautenii*, commonly called Zimbabwe balsa wood, which is rather like the bulbous baobab in shape, but smaller. The wood, when dry, is extremely light. It is used by the local people for the carving of masks. The nuts are very hard, look like Brazil nuts but taste like hazel nuts.

Elephants chisel bark from trees then strip it off with their trunks.

Opposite: An elephant bull luxuriates in a bath on the Dete vlei.

The elephants will take in dozens of them at a time, digesting only the thin outer skin. The nut itself is so hard that an elephant cannot easily crush it between its powerful molars. I have often found a pile of elephant dung up to ten miles away from the nearest Mugongo tree grove and containing as many as 20 or 30 nuts. These, when broken, yield a very tasty kernel inside, and many is the hour I have sat with my guests around a pile of elephant dung breaking open the Mugongo nuts for the kernel. This is another example of seed distribution and habitat creation by elephants, sometimes called ' Africa's greatest gardeners'.

After a long hot thirsty march through the bush I am often relieved to come across the wild Morning Glory *(Ipomea shirambensis)*. At a depth of some two feet or so this plant has potato-like tubers. To obtain copious quantities of a clear tasteless liquid, lightly scrape away the outer skin with its latex-like layer, cut into slices and chew. I am sure that the bushmen hunters of the Kalahari would have been familiar with this plant as a source of life saving moisture when they hunted this area in days gone by.

I am always amazed at the knowledge of elephants, particularly when it comes to knowing which plants to eat at which season - and the best times of the day to harvest them. It is noticeable that during the month of September, which is probably the month during which the nutritional levels of the food supply is at its lowest ebb, that the elephants will break off large truncheons of the Kalahari Sand Rain Tree *(Loncocarpus nelsii)*.

I was told many years ago by the distinguished botanist, John Rushworth, who worked in Hwange National Park, that the crude level proteins of this plant approach approximately 30% at this time of the year, representing the highest crude protein level of any plant in the Hwange National Park, a level

even higher than the grazing grasses at the height of the rainy season. Commonly one will see an elephant break off a truncheon and crush the bough between his molars to extract all the juices and spit out the splintered remnants.

From time to time elephants will utilise the 'rubber' tree *(Diplorinchus condylocarpon)*. This shrub, which never attains a great height in Hwange due to the attention of elephants and the effects of fire and frost, produces a rubbery latex which can be useful for making bird traps. This particular plant is also a favoured plant specie for the endangered black rhino.

The two most common types of brachystegia, boehmii and spiciformis are utilised quite widely by elephants, particularly the former which is a favoured plant species. Often when I am out on a track I will strip off the inner bark of brachystegia and give this to the people with me, some of whom may be thirsty,

It looks rough and insensitive, but an elephants' skin is equipped with touch receptors which enable it to feel and pinpoint an insect bite.

to make into a little ball to chew, demonstrating how this activates the saliva glands. These brachystegias, or Msasa, as they are commonly called, are amongst the most useful plants in the bush. They are long fibred, and it is possible to end up with a very long and strong piece of fibre with which one can make a plaited rope so strong that people have been known to make an emergency vehicle towing rope out of it.

There are, of course, a variety of other uses varying from dental floss, urgent bush replacements for shoelaces, belts, gun belts, or anything where one would require rope, string or thread. I have used this before now to bind the ankle of an unfortunate person who had tripped over and sprained his ankle and in the absence of a bandage it held up very firmly.

I have always enjoyed showing my clients these plants as I believe it helps to give an holistic view of the total environment. Life after all, even on the Hwange Estate, is not centred solely on elephants.

For example, when tracking them you could be distracted by the incessant chattering of a Greater Honeyguide, a small drab looking bird. Once you indicate your desire to follow by tapping on a tree, you will be led in a series of short chattering flights to a tree or log where the bird will remain conspicuously silent. A search of the tree will indicate a beehive. There is an old African tradition that when the hive is robbed, a small quantity of larvae should be left for the bird to eat, otherwise at some time in the future it will lead the 'robber' into danger - a snake or a leopard perhaps.

"Anyone who cannot relate to the earth and who has a disturbed relationship with nature will suffer from acute spiritual and emotional imbalance. Nature, with its fixed laws, provides support and gives direction. Nature's changing seasons communicate a meaning to us".- Professor Dr. M Rock, University of Mainz.

The Hwange Estate today has become an unique, world-famous elephant sanctuary. It is positioned on the eastern extremity of the ancient Kalahari desert system and shares a common boundary with Zimbabwe's vast Hwange National Park. To explain how this has come about I want to take you back to an ancient time when our Kalahari woodland world was created.

Dramatic climactic changes have taken place here over a period of at least five million years. After the harsh, dry conditions of the Pliocene and Pleistocene Ages (between five and two million years ago) the earth's climate began a new series of dramatic cycles, the result of swings between Sun/Earth access and the various ice ages. Every 20-30,000 years the Kalahari climate alternated between being dry and windy or cool and wet. It was under these conditions that the Kalahari dune systems were created. Some are half a million years old; some as recent as 10,000 years.

Between 40,000 and 26,000 years ago a cool, wet period produced a network of swamps, rivers and lakes. There were teak trees then, amongst considerable forest cover, but the temperatures on average were 5-15° cooler than today. Rainfall was 50-100% greater.

At this time there was almost certainly a greater diversity of animals and plants than we have today. But the Kalahari area and its diversity of climate and vegetation would already have been familiar territory for more than three million years to our own African Elephant *(Loxodonta Africana)*, one of the greatest genetically unchanged time travellers of all.

15,000 years ago came the end of the last maximum glacial period in the Northern Hemisphere. In the South, once again, it began to dry. The lakes disappeared and the last of the principal

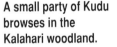

A small party of Kudu browses in the Kalahari woodland.

calcrete deposits, or lime precipitates formed by seasonal inundation, were laid down.

The hot, dry, violent winds which blew from the Kalahari Desert in the west, relentlessly carrying particles of sand before them, ceased 10,000 years ago. The force of the winds created friction between the sand particles so that each grain took on a round shape. These rounded particles were deposited layer by layer upon sand dunes which in some places piled more than 100 metres high. Nature has an awesome power, and this massive body of moving sand was transported from more than a thousand kilometres away.

What was once a panorama of bare, red decomposed sandstone valleys and sand dunes with howling wind and driving sand is now a peaceful scene of stately Kalahari woodland savannah, interspersed with grassy valleys, open

areas of calcrete soils and Leadwood (*Combretum imberbe*) trees. The sandy nature of the area means that the 600 mm annual rainfall is generally soaked up by the porous sand. A high proportion of this is held in the top two metres by the tightly packed sand grains and provides moisture for the many shallow-rooted plants. The larger, slow-growing, hardwood trees have extensive root systems. With as much as 80% of their plant biomass below ground they are able to tap into the stored moisture at greater depths.

Over the centuries the untapped water has gently filtered through, some authorities believe, to an impermeable water table, which may be as deep as 100 metres or more.

Today the only areas that hold surface water occur within the relatively few and widely-spaced calcrete deposits. These "pans" or waterholes have been made almost seep-proof by the elephants and other game through their wallowing and are the only receptacles of rain water. In a normal year all are dry by September due to evaporation and consumption by the wildlife. Any rivers that may have existed west of the Gwayi River were covered over by the driven sand thousands of years ago.

In more recent geological time, subterranean upheavals occurred causing faulting of the rock bodies below. Locally the most significant fault gave birth to the Dete vlei (a valley or shallow grassy depression) where water, forced up from the depths, passed through the underlying coal bodies to the surface in the form of hot sulphur springs. Slightly north of the Dete vlei the Gwayi River carves its course through the granite hills, whilst in the south is situated the broad water-filled Sikumi vlei.

Thus, for thousands of years until the present day, (when man modified the habitat by the provision of pumped underground water), the vast area to the south and west was mainly a summer grazing area. As the pans dried up, the diverse wildlife used to fall back for water onto the Dete and Sikumi vleis and the Gwayi River farther north.

Elephant Hunting

From time immemorial, the little Kalahari Bushmen used the Dete vlei area and the surrounding woodland as an important hunting area. The forest became their living larder in the summer between November to late April during the rainy season, when the game came to drink the water in the pans.

Later in the year on the Dete and nearby Sikumi vlei, as competition amongst the game for food and water and the presence of bushman hunters increased, the game would move towards the bigger rivers such as the Gwayi and Zambezi further to the north and east. The Bushman were subsistence hunter-gatherers, whose sole pre-occupation was finding food. They therefore presented no threat to the elephants.

With their bows and poison-tipped arrows they killed what they needed and ate it. Their varied diet included kudu, eland, zebra, tortoises, birds, hares and ostrich eggs as well as berries, bulbs and wild honey.

The Portuguese traded in ivory in other parts of Zimbabwe as early as the 15th century, but it is doubtful that Hwange elephant tusks ever reached the commer-cial ivory market until the 19th century and the advent of the Victorian hunters and traders.

Commercial hunting of elephants for ivory started with the arrival of Mzilikazi, a Zulu general, who had fled the wrath of his warrior-king Tshaka for insubordination and cattle theft. He finally settled with his followers in what became known as Matabeleland. In 1838 he was proclaimed the first Ndebele king

Bush hunters

and set up his new capital in Bulawayo, 200 kms to the south of Hwange. His arrival stimulated a growing trickle of European visitors from south of the Limpopo River who were primarily interested in hunting and trading and who traded ivory for barter goods such as muskets, cloth and beads.

In former times the Zulus in Natal, who were noted for their formidable courage, were known to kill elephants with spears after running in and hamstringing them with large axes. However, the availability of muzzle loaders no longer necessitated this risky practice. In Matabeleland, Mzilikazi dispatched his own skilled hunters to his hunting preserve in what today forms part of the Hwange National Park.

The most celebrated of the Victorian hunters and writers in Africa was Frederick Courtney Selous (pronounced Seloo), whose father was the Chairman of the London Stock Exchange. As a young man in his early twenties in 1872, Selous obtained permission to hunt from King Lobengula, who had succeeded his father King Mzilikazi in 1859.

For Selous and hundreds of other 19th century hunters elephants were the principal quarry. Whites hunted the Hwange area, a controlled royal hunting preserve from which Ndebele commoners were excluded, with the consent of the king on a

Bringing ivory tusks to the wagon trains
(Thomas Baines)

Frederick Courtney Selous

tribute basis. Permission to hunt had to be obtained from Lobengula, Mzilikazi's son until 1893, when the British colonised the country.

Despite the heavy toll exacted upon the elephants, the execution was not as great as was to follow in the 20th century. One reason for this was that hunting in the 19th century was seasonal. The menace of Malaria meant that hunting could only be conducted for six months of the year in the dry months, between May and October. Additionally, because of the presence of the tsetse fly, much of the hunting had to be carried out on foot since to bring horses into this environment would almost certainly prove fatal to them.

The hunters came up in wagons which they would leave just outside the tsetse fly belt together with their horses and oxen. Sometimes they would ride if they were fortunate enough to possess what were called 'salted horses'. These animals had previously been bitten by the tsetse fly and had developed an immunity to it. Possession of highly prized 'salted horses' greatly facilitated elephant hunting.

Usually a hunting party consisted of one or two white hunters and twenty or so bearers following behind with the

The elephant gun owned by F.C. Selous
Source: National Archives Exhibits collection

baggage. They ate what they shot, but they would carry basic commodities such as grain, coffee and sugar.

A typical hunting trip would last six months. The professional hunters were hunting for ivory but the more successful would only have killed a couple of hundred elephants each during a hunting career. (By comparison with today's population reduction exercises in National Parks, involving the use of aircraft, vehicles, radios and high powered rifles the number of elephants killed was relatively small).

Selous visited the exact area where today the Presidential Herd of Elephants now roams. His graphic account, published 120 years ago in "A Hunter's Wanderings in Africa", illustrates the excitement and dangers of elephant hunting in the last century. This hunt takes place in an area on the Hwange Estate which I know intimately. I am now associated with the descendents of the very same elephants that he so persistently slew and affirm that the cruel persecution of these wonderful animals here, is now but a historical memory. Selous is worth quoting at length:

"Our camp where I had buried the ivory was situated some considerable distance down the valley, and about eight or ten

Ndebele warriors
Source: National Archives

miles from the Sinangas on the night we reached Dete. Whilst sleeping there we heard elephants drinking at a waterhole not far up the valley and at the first dawn of day, after having had a cup of hot coffee, we went and took up the spoor. The elephants, a fine troop of eight or ten bulls, had been feeding quietly along all night through the large open grassy forests, which bordered Dete, always heading however towards the Sinangas, where we guessed they were bent upon standing during the heat of the day. It was however not an hour or so past midday, as they pursued a circuitous course backwards and forwards that our conjectures were confirmed and we entered the thick bush.

About an hour later we came up with them standing some fifty yards away on our right under a clump of Camelthorn trees and in a rather open place, compared with the general density of the surrounding jungle. Besides the small troop of bulls we had followed, and which were nearest to us, there was a very large herd of cows standing just beyond which, as we had not crossed their spoor, had probably drunk at Sikumi, a waterhole not many miles distant, and come to this rendezvous from the other side.

Tasting a hasty gulp of water we at once walked towards them. As we advanced, the slight rustling of the bushes must have attracted the attention of one of the bulls, for he raised his trunk high in the air and made a few steps forward. "I'll take him, and do you fire at the one with the long white tusks on the left," whispered W. "Right you are!" was the reply. The next moment we fired. I just had time to see my elephant fall to his knees, when he was hidden by the troop of cows, that, awakened from their sleep by the shots, had, not knowing exactly where the danger lay, came rushing towards us in a mass, one or two of them trumpeting and others making a sort of rumbling noise. Seizing our second guns and shouting lustily we again pulled the trigger. Our Hottentot boy, John,

and five of our bearers who still carried guns also fired on which the herd turned and went off at right angles, enveloped in a cloud of dust. My gun had only snapped the cap, but my bearer, to whom I threw it back, thinking in the noise and hurry that it was discharged, reloaded it on top of the old charge, a fact which I only found out to my sorrow later on.

The cloud of sand and dust raised by the panic stricken elephants was at first so thick that we could distinguish nothing, but running behind them, I soon made out the bull I had wounded, which I recognised by the length and shape of his tusks. He was evidently hard hit, and being unable to keep up with the herd, he turned out and went off alone, but he was joined almost immediately by four old cows, all with small insignificant tusks, and instead of running away, they walked along quite slowly, first in front of, and then, behind him as if to encourage him. Seeing how severely he was wounded, I at once went after him accompanied only by my two gun carriers, Nuta and Balamoya, W. and the rest of the bearers going on after the troop. My bull was going so slowly that I had no difficulty in threading my way through the bushes and getting in front of him, which I did in order to get a broadside shot as he passed me. One of the four cows that still accompanied him walked along carrying her head high and her tail straight in the air and kept constantly turning from side to side. "That cow will bother us; shoot her," said Nuta - and I wish I had taken his advice - but her tusks were so small and the bull seemed so very far gone that I thought it would be a waste of ammunition. I therefore waited till he was a little in front of where I stood and then gave him a bullet at very close quarters just behind the shoulder, and as I thought, exactly in the right place. Nevertheless he continued his walk as if he had not felt it. Reloading the same gun I ran behind him holding it before me in both hands, ready to raise at a moment's notice. The four cows being some 20 yards in advance, I shouted, hoping he would turn. The sound of my voice had the desired effect for he at once raised his ears and swung himself round, or rather was in the act of doing so, for immediately his ears went up. My gun was at my shoulder and as soon as he presented his broadside I fired, on which he turned again and went crashing through the bushes at a trot. I thought that this was the last spasmodic rush and that he would fall before going very far. So, giving the gun back to Nuta to reload I was running after him with my eyes fixed on the quivering bushes as they closed behind him, when suddenly, the trunk of another elephant was whirled round almost literally above my head and a short sharp scream

of rage thrilled through me, making the blood tingle down to the very tips of my fingers. It was one of the wretched old cows, who had, lain in wait for me beside a dense patch of bush. Even had my gun been in my hands I should scarcely have had time to fire, so close was she upon me. But as it was, both my bearers were some 15 yards behind and the only thing I could do was to run. How I got away I scarcely knew. I bounded over and through thorn bushes, which in cold blood I should have judged impenetrable, but I was urged on by the short piercing screams which repeated in quick succession seemed to make the whole air vibrate and by the fear of finding myself encircled

On the Elephant Marsh Shire River
Source: Africa and it's exploration as told by it's experience
National Archives of Zimbabwe.

by the trunk or transfixed by the tusk of the enraged animal. After a few seconds, when I do not think she pursued me a 100 yards although it seemed an age, the screaming ceased. During the chase the elephant was so close behind me that looking over my shoulder was impossible and all that I did was to dash forwards springing from side to side so as to hinder her from getting hold of me and it was only when the trumpeting suddenly stopped that I knew I was out of her reach. I was bare-legged as I always am when hunting on foot and my only garment before the beast charged was a flannel shirt. Now I stood almost in 'puris naturalibus' but for my hat, a leather belt I wore round my waist and about three parts of my shirt had been torn off by the bushes and I doubt that there was a square inch of skin left uninjured on the front of my body."

Whenever hunters move into an area and disturb elephants through shooting, the latter very soon abandon their home range for safer places. It is sometimes several months before they will return. In the 19th century, sparse human occupation of the Hwange region left a vast vacant area into which the elephants could disperse and stay out of harm's way. This also placed a natural limitation on the numbers of elephants killed.

With the passing of the Victorian adventurers, the pressure on elephants for their ivory and as objects of sport hunting increased. Early in the 20th century, motor vehicles were introduced and this made hunting even easier.

At that time there were few game laws and wildlife was generally viewed as a never-ending resource. Little thought was given to conservation. Elephant and lion hunters were particularly admired. They themselves perpetuated the myth of their bravery, having themselves photographed astride the moribund bodies of their victims and as if to emphasise their courage, and having their trophies preserved in snarling poses by a burgeoning taxidermist trade.

Authors, some of whom never even visited 'the Dark Continent', wrote the most graphic and inaccurate accounts of the savagery of African animals. Quotes such as "I felled the brute" or "the wicked beast fell dead at my feet" abound in pre-First World War game hunting stories. Later, in the 1920s, big bull elephants with massive tusks sweeping to the ground, allegedly the patriarchs of massive herds, graduated to being described as 'rogues'. Most of the descriptions demonstrated complete ignorance of the true nature and social behaviour of these gentle animals.

New farms were opened up with disastrous results for the game. Cattle farming could not take place in districts inhabited by the tsetse fly and a massive and systematic elimination of the fly's hosts was therefore embarked upon. For forty years hunters were employed to kill every animal they could find. In the process of this useless exercise millions of wild animals perished.

But a dramatic event with far-reaching benefits for wildlife in the country occurred in 1928 with the establishment of the

One of the first motor cars in Zimbabwe

Nation's first national park at Hwange. In the years between the two world wars there began to be a growing realisation that wildlife was finite. A progressive body of legislation aimed at wildlife protection was enacted so that hunting throughout the country became increasingly controlled on a licence system. Ownership of wildlife was invested in the State and whilst this was well intentioned, it had the effect of diminishing the value to farmers of wildlife on their land because, apart from eating the game, they were not allowed to utilise it commercially for their own benefit. (This deficiency was later corrected in 1975). It did, however, put an end to the ivory trade, as only sport hunting on a rigorously controlled basis was permitted. Large scale commercial safari hunting in the country was at that time unknown.

Until further parks were established after the Second World War, the only elephants outside Hwange National Park could be found in the communal tribal areas controlled by district commissioners or on pockets of State Land.

Certain animals such as rhino and cheetah were declared 'Royal Game', that is not to be killed under any circumstances but any farmer wishing to kill an elephant on his own land had to purchase a licence. Until the legislation was amended in 1975, most hunting of elephant for fun was carried out by government officials, often under the excuse of protecting tribal area crops. Any ivory recovered as a result of these activities had to be handed over to the State. On State Land other government officials, so-called VIPs and politicians using a variety of dubious excuses, were able to hunt elephants without licence.

Reflecting on man's desire to dominate without respect for the magnificence of the natural world

Johnny Uys

Part of the present-day Hwange Estate is a block of State Land which constitutes the core area of our Presidential Elephants' home range. This land was not included within the boundaries of the Hwange National Park and, unlike all other land in the area, was not transferred to private ownership. Ted Davison, the first Warden of Hwange National Park, with foresight in the 1930s, proposed that a 'game corridor' should be left for resident animals of the Park to obtain drinking water from the Gwayi River in times of severe drought. As it turned out, game from the Park never used this corridor for the purpose intended, primarily because the National Parks Department themselves embarked on their own successful programme of drilling boreholes for water.

No Man's Land

Sadly, the elephants within the corridor were not officially considered to be part of the protected population of the Park. Because they occasionally entered the neighbouring communal area they were treated, if anything, as a nuisance. As a result they were mercilessly hunted. For example, there was the excuse that they were crop raiders or that young game rangers needed training in elephant killing or that guests of the old government should be given free sport hunting. The situation was worsened by the lack of status of all wildlife on state land and it is little wonder that the poor elephants lived in a perpetual state of fear right up until 1972. To add to the their difficulties, a large human population was building up in the nearby communal land to the east and north, effectively cutting off any long-term retreat from the hunters.

In the latter days the farms in the area, mostly of 6,00-8,000 acres, were used for logging and were heavily hunted. At the time we acquired our land, it had become desecrated. There were no big trees left. The hardwoods had been sold to the saw-milling companies and most of the game had disappeared.

Elephants would only pass through on their way to the National Park or on their return to the State land, invariably at night. They were unapproachable because everybody used to shoot at them. There were no large bulls and the cows were all small because the bigger ones had been killed. The area had virtually become a no-man's land killing ground.

The awful free-for-all in no man's land spluttered to an end in 1970 with the development of the Hwange Safari Lodge by Zimbabwe Sun Hotels, a subsidiary of Delta Corporation, fortunately a strongly conservation-minded organisation.

The idea of creating a large private sanctuary with facilities for tourists outside the government-controlled National Park system was revolutionary. It was envisaged that the Lodge would, for the first time in the history of the country, encourage foreign visitors to partake in game-viewing and photographic safaris. This development, conveniently situated between Victoria Falls and Lake Kariba, pioneered organised tourism in Zimbabwe.Leases were negotiated over part of the Sikumi Forest and State Land and two adjoining farms were purchased, making a single block of approximately 150 square kilometres.

Due to the heavy slaughter of all game in the past there was no immediate prospect of the sanctuary being used for photographic safaris when the Hwange Safari Lodge opened in 1972, but at least the tide had turned. Both then and now parties are taken on safari into the whole conservation area which includes the 14,000 square kilometre Hwange National Park.

Hwange Safari Lodge

With great enthusiasm the developers searched for the best qualified man in Africa to develop the concession into a game park and to set up a team of safari guides to escort guests on photographic, educational and walking safaris on the newly proclaimed Hwange Estate. No man on the African continent had better credentials than Johnny Uys.

A secretion from the temporal gland is thought to indicate stress.

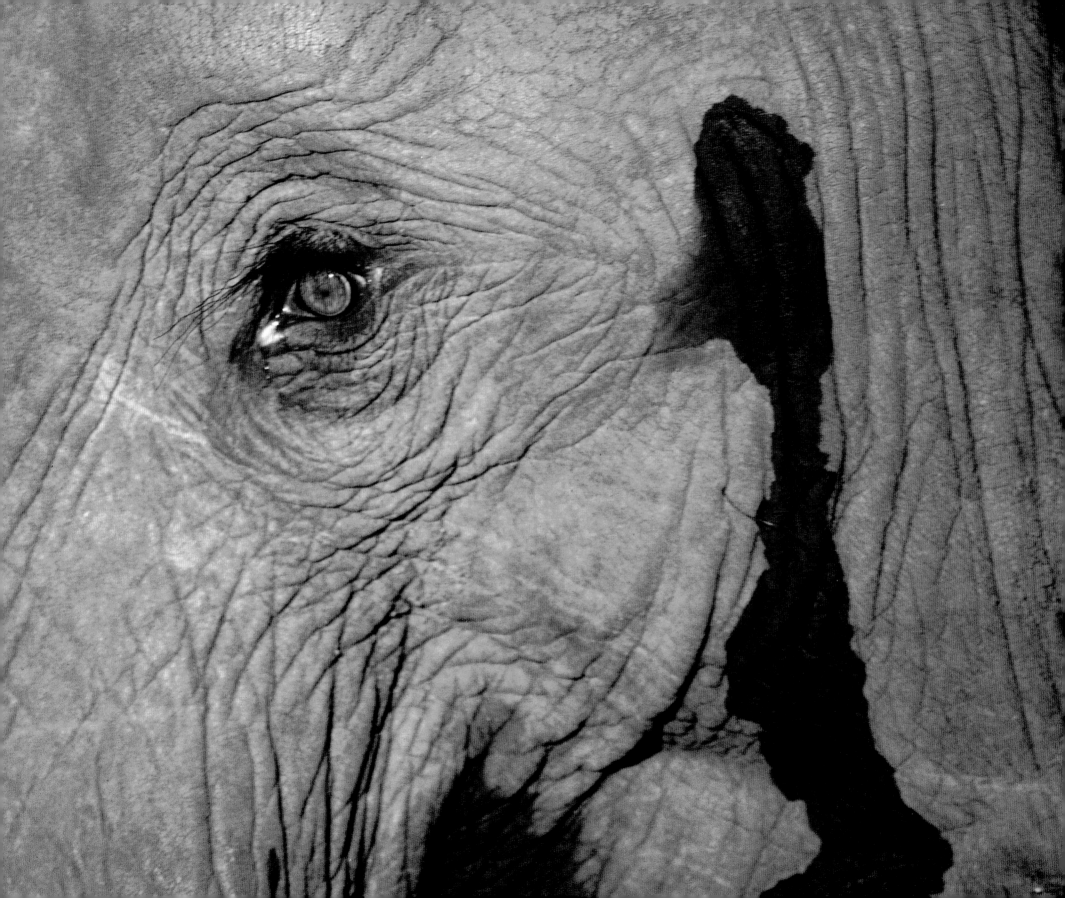

Johnny Uys Recruited

Uys was recruited from his position as Chief Game Warden in Zambia and took up his post in 1970. He was a man of great practical experience, incredible knowledge of the bush and its wildlife and he had the necessary strength and drive to do the job. In Africa today, Zimbabwean Safari Guides are reckoned to be second to none. Their high standards, the emphasis on an holistic approach, that is, an interest in botany, ornithology, entomology, zoology and bush-lore and a high degree of professionalism are one of the great legacies of Johnny Uys.

Yet the Estate in those early days was so run down and depleted that, although Johnny was one of the most skilled of all bush men, on more than one occasion when he took parties out on a safari, they saw not a single mammal. Today, the miracle is that you can see a wide variety of animals anywhere on the Estate from the elephants, lions, leopards, wild dogs, various species of antelopes and many smaller mammals.

Johnny Uys had little formal education and left school before the age of 16. Amongst his early jobs was that of a grader driver with the Roads Department working in the National Parks in Zambia. Such was his enthusiasm for the wilderness and all things wild, he was soon absorbed into the Game Department of Northern Rhodesia where he excelled himself. Amongst other things, Johnny became a very proficient botanist and it is recorded that experts from Kew Gardens travelled to Zambia to interview him on aspects of botany in the parks where he worked.

When Johnny came to the Hwange Estate he was initially disliked, but later grudgingly respected, by the local white population living in the railway community of Dete because of his strenuous and successful efforts against their poaching activities. In those early days of Hwange we had very few kudu, or any other antelope for that matter, and each animal was very precious. One morning, Johnny woke up to find a set of kudu horns and a wet, dripping, bloody skin nailed to the gate of the space surrounding his house. In due course he discovered who the culprit was and had him arrested.

One of Johnny's principal aims was to increase the game carrying capacity of the Hwange Estate and he worked tirelessly developing forest roads, providing boreholes and building the large dam which still bears his name. He was also a skilled camp builder. The original bush camp tree-house that he built still rests solidly in a large umtshibi tree in the grounds of what is now Sable Valley Lodge.

Wild Life Returns

Uys tackled his new job with enthusiasm and in a very short time the basic infrastructure started to emerge. Imperceptibly there were increasing signs that the wildlife was returning and, in particular, it was noticeable that the Sable antelope were becoming more tolerant to the presence of vehicles.

Johnny Uys had lived most of his life with big game. Through his ability he rose rapidly up the ranks of the Zambian Game Department, acquiring a considerable international reputation on the way. His duties had included elephant culling, and he had been required to kill at least 2,000 elephants. Apart from his ability with a rifle, he was a highly skilled self-taught mechanic, who repaired and modified all his own vehicle and tractor engines and borehole pumping engines.

Of even greater consequence, he was an outstandingly good bush man. Totally fearless, he loved to track elephants on foot and get his clients really close to them - on some occasions too close! Whenever an elephant objected to his proximity and made a rush or threatening gesture, he would bang two sticks together and this normally had the effect of halting the aggressor. If this technique was insufficient, he would whack the large beast with his stick and drive it off. As a back-up,

Surprise probably caused this aggressive posture by a bull elephant.

Inset: The late Johnny Uys

he always carried the heavy calibre rifle that had seen him through many years of faithful service and which he would steadfastly refuse to unsling from his shoulder except in an emergency. Following behind Johnny on one of his "Discovery Trails", one always had a feeling of great security. He was so confident, so wise, that one soon felt a sense of his infallibility - immortality almost. The last occasion on which I spoke to him about this method of guiding and its apparent risks, he said with complete sincerity, "Man, I know these elephants". I believed him.

Tragic Loss

Some six weeks later, Johnny was leading a small party of German visitors on an early morning walk when he picked up the fresh spoor of one of the two breeding herds. On this occasion there was a bull accompanying the group. There was an easterly breeze as usual and the herd was moving in the same direction. Elephants rely very much on the wind to carry scent to them. With the history of hunting pressure to which the group had become accustomed, they no doubt used their ingrained habit of monitoring the air. In a short time the party caught up with the elephants which bunched up and faced them with trunks up, obviously aware of the human presence. Using his bush craft, Johnny worked his way around the wind, approaching the herd so as to give his clients every opportunity to use their cine cameras to record the dramatic event. Had he been alone, no doubt he could have quite easily approached the elephant herd very closely. With a party of untrained city dwellers this was impossible. The noise and movement was just too much of an irritation and one of the cows charged the party. Johnny rushed forward, picking up a stout branch as he did so and struck the enraged cow on her body. Confused, she stopped and stood broadside on to him. For a second Johnny seemed to be contemplating his next move when the larger bull, unseen by

him, brushed past the cow's rump and, with head lowered, knocked Johnny to the ground. While the elephant was on its knees and trying to gore him, Johnny managed to load his rifle and fire into the huge head. On being hit by the bullet, the shocked animal stood up and then set upon its helpless victim with renewed rage. At this stage the visitors who had been filming the whole incident, decided to decamp. When asked later why they had continued filming, their spokesman replied, "We thought it was part of the show."

Colleagues reacting to the news hurried to the spot and were met by an unimaginable sight. Johnny had been severely assaulted by the elephants and it appeared that all had joined in digging up the soil, and excavating a trench about 20 metres long into which they had pushed his body, throwing sand and branches over it in an act of uncontrolled emotion. They then ran off at speed, heading for the sanctuary of the National Park.

Game Rangers were summoned from the National Park and an urgent debate took place. Would these animals, having killed a human, kill again? Would they get over the incident and totally forget it? Nobody could be certain, so a decision was taken to err on the side of caution and a follow-up was ordered. The panic-stricken herd had run for 18 kms and was found by the rangers in a thicket where they were surrounded and all 13 members of the family shot.

Thus ended the blackest day in the history of Hwange Estate. We had in one day lost Johnny Uys, at 47 in the prime of his life, his vast store of knowledge and bush lore unrecorded. In wildlife circles Johnny was a living legend. The legend lives on. But we also lost one third of our elephant population.

The sun that set on that awful August day in 1973 closed a chapter.

Life had to go on and it was left to those who remained to ensure the future well-being of of the wildlife in our newly created sanctuary. The difficult task of picking up the pieces and carrying on fell upon the shoulders of Johnny's assistant and good friend from the Zambian days, John Rutlege.

Shortly afterwards, John decided to return to the commercial world and I shall always be grateful to him for recommending me to be his successor as Game Manager of the Hwange Estate. I was immensely excited but also fearful of the awesome responsibility this would entail. Living in the shadow of my illustrious predecessor was not easy in the beginning, but I resolved to devote myself to the task.

Learning about Wildlife

Logically, I should never had any interest in coming into close contact with elephants. As a child I used to listen with awed fascination to my grandparents talking about the old Victorian adventurers, many of whom they had encountered in their early days. Invariably, the discussion would lead to some epic and horrific hunting incident, no doubt embellished in the telling, involving the ferocity of elephants, lions or buffaloes. Particularly vivid in the annals of my family was my great uncle, Hans Lee. A noted bush man, he was engaged by Lord Randolph Churchill as a hunter and guide in the 1890s. One year he was employed by King Lobengula to hunt giraffe for their tails, which were to be made into ceremonial switches and which the king sent to Swaziland to pay for brides.

My mother was so conditioned by her fear of elephants that the first time, aged 12, that I ever saw elephant dung in the road on which we were driving, to my great disappointment, she screeched on the brakes of the car, turned round and abandoned the journey. With hindsight I reckon that dung was over a week old! To this day my mother finds it hard to fathom my infatuation with elephants.

An infatuation with elephants!

Heads up, tails out as elephants flee.

I am a fourth generation Zimbabwean. My great-grand parents are buried in this country and I grew up and went to a bush school in Matabeleland. My father had a chain of remote trading stores. During school holidays from the age of ten, and armed with a .22 rifle, I used to roam the bush shooting anything that moved. My grandparents had a big ranch and encouraged me to go out at an early age. My friends were the Ndebele kids whose families worked for my grandparents and who were great little hunters. I could speak the language, which was an advantage, but they had a special knowledge of wildlife

and the environment, (tracking, bushlore, trees, birds, animals and insects) which they readily passed on to me. As I grew older so the calibre of my rifles increased, but the basis of what I know about wildlife today was learned from these friends.

Even before I left school I was considered to be an experienced hunter, having shot a great many animals. My burning ambition was to go to Kenya and become a professional hunter. But above all I wanted to prove my manhood to myself by confronting and killing my first elephant. The elephants had long been driven out of the ranching areas of the Plumtree district where I was brought up and as it turned out, I was already 19 by the time I saw my first elephant, ironically, being much older than many of the bright young people we take on safari, or some of the city-reared boys who I train as learner guides today.

Against Sport Hunting

After I left school I joined the government service and rose to the dizzy rank of District Officer. One of my responsibilities was to deal with problem animals and it was at that time, that I turned completely against hunting for sport.

I had to shoot some lions which were killing cattle on the Mazowe river in the north eastern part of the country. They had been causing havoc in the territory for some time. A number of myths had grown up among the terrorised local people that they had eyes that shone like fire and if they stared at you, you would melt! As described, they were made to sound the size of buffaloes. When word got out that I had despatched the lions, hundreds of joyful people streamed out to view the dead 'demons'. There were women with babies on their backs, some giggling, some crying. Amongst the noise and confusion and people poking and kicking the dead lions, I felt a sudden revulsion. I reflected that lions had hunted in these parts for centuries and were now reduced to surviving on domestic cattle, because their traditional prey had been displaced by an exploding human population. In that moment my enjoyment of sport hunting came to an end. That was it. I was 21 years of age.

I continued my career as a District Officer and later, as part of my duties protecting tribal crops when I did shoot my first bull elephant, I was filled with remorse and sadness. The realisation of my youthful ambition to kill an elephant, under the circumstances, proved totally anticlimactic.

My boyhood dream of working in the safari industry was still burning, only I no longer wished to kill rather to observe, learn, photograph and share my knowledge with others. The creation of the Hwange Safari Lodge and the new direction in non-hunting, photographic tourism which Zimbabwe took at that time provided an ideal opportunity and I have been deeply involved with it ever since.

First Encounter

It is said that elephants have long memories. I have a clear vision of my first encounter with the small, original group of cows. It was in an acacia grove on the Dete vlei near where the Hwange Safari Lodge is today. It was such a fleeting glimpse as about a dozen animals stampeded in panic across the track with terrified little calves, seemingly very vulnerable in the blur of movement and dust, tucked between their mothers' pillar-like legs which drove up and down like large pistons. In no time at all the trumpeting, squealing group, ears erect and tails stretched out horizontally had disappeared through the grove like a violent dust storm.

To this day I am always saddened at the sight of these wonderful animals rushing away in fear and often in the deathly silence that follows, I am left wondering at the cruelty of man to cause such panic. There is also a poignant symbolism in a silent, empty landscape where a moment ago there were elephants and then, suddenly, none. I sometimes wish that

elephants could be made aware of their awesome power and that, instead of fleeing, they would turn on their persecutors en masse and send them packing back to their cities, rifles and all.

Initially, certain officials continued to enter Hwange Estates and shoot the bull elephants. When I protested, I was invariably told that the individuals were merely doing their job and that the animals had been tracked down after raiding crops in the adjacent village of Dete or the communal area. It took some time for the situation to be redressed and eventually all shooting was halted. Needless to say, we were not very popular in the district.

Dete was established as a large railway village to serve the Victoria Falls railway line. In those days there were many rifle-owning people who had viewed the Estate land as a common hunting ground from which they could replenish their larders. This practice took some halting but, after a series of successful prosecutions for trespass and poaching, we managed to get on top of the situation. Again we were unpopular.

The Hwange Estate sanctuary had been set up to support a tourist industry that was not exactly flourishing at that time. This was probably fortuitous, as with my very small staff I was able to continue with the necessary primary development There was much work to be done establishing permanent water points, as there are no rivers in this area of flat Kalahari woodland, all water supplies had to be pumped from boreholes and deposited into seep-proof clay pans. There were roads and firebreaks to be cut and maintained, anti-poaching teams to be established, and camps to be built for the expected tourists.

The sanctuary was established with a view to encouraging all existing game species which included Sable antelope, kudu and other species which we had introduced such as impala, wildebeeste, zebra and white rhino. All of these tasks necessitated many hours in the veld every day. This gave me a wonderful opportunity to monitor the elephant population.

In those early days a clear strategy for game utilisation on the Estate had not evolved. To my subsequent regret, it was at first thought that a multiple land use policy including commercial safari hunting represented sound land utilisation. In time, as I got to know the elephants as individuals, I determined that there could no longer be a place for hunting of any kind on the Estate and I committed myself to do all that I could to bring some sort of peace to these creatures and call a halt to the slaughter which had been going on for hundreds of years.

A fine specimen of male Sable antelope. These animals have increased greatly on the Estate.

Today at Hwange we have one of the densest populations of elephants anywhere in Africa and our herd of Presidential Elephants is now over 300 strong. Twenty years ago we identified 22 elephants in two families on the Estate. At that time they were, as I have already indicated, extremely nervous.

Initial Contacts

Apart from the routine work to open up the Estate for game viewing such as creating tracks and firebreaks and ensuring that the boreholes were in order, my main priority was to try to acclimatise the elephants to our presence.

It is always difficult to approach elephants in vehicles in the heavy woodland of Hwange. The easiest method is to catch them in the open areas around the waterholes. Unfortunately, elephants that have been heavily hunted will only drink at night and it therefore became necessary for me to sit at their favourite waterhole of Kanondo after dark and hope that they would arrive. These vigils, listening to the sounds of the veldt whether insects, animals or nocturnal birds, were a source of great relaxation. They were my umbilical cord with Mother Nature.

By listening you can detect the imminence of approaching elephants in the blackness. It might be just a twig snapping, an exhaled breath or the thud of a ball of dung as it hits the ground. Elephants can be extraordinarily quiet. Sometimes the first indication I would have of their arrival would be the sound of water splashing as the excess drops fell from their mouths back into the pond. Sometimes it would be the more subtle scraping of feet in the sand nearby as they entered the mineral lick. I would always sit very still in the vehicle and wait for them to investigate me. Although they were more bold at night, they were still very suspicious and would circle the vehicle with trunks held high in an attempt to pick up and identify the scent. Fortunately, fuel fumes tend to mask the smell of humans.

As I became more familiar with my small family of elephants I was fascinated by the differing physical characteristics of the four mature cows. It was clear that the reason these animals had not so far been shot was because they were still young and carried very small or deformed tusks or, as in the case of one cow, no tusks at all. She was the oldest animal and presumably owed her continued existence to the fact that she was born tuskless. In normal situations a cow elephant of 20 to 25 years of age would not rank very highly in the family, but she was the oldest surviving female in 1974 and consequently the

mantle of leadership fell upon her. Initially she was called the "Tuskless Cow". Much later this was changed to 'Inkosikazi'. In the Ndebele language a lady of high or royal rank is an Inkosikazi. The name seemed most appropriate and she has always behaved accordingly.

Another young female in the group, who appeared to be about 18 years old, had a deformed left tusk which, instead of curving forward and upwards, curved in the opposite direction towards her chest. Her tusks were about nine inches long. This elephant became known as "Skew Tusk" and over the

years has become one of the most photographed and easily identified elephants on Hwange Estate. From the start, she was aggressive. Obviously into her short life had been packed incidents which had taught her not to trust man.

Another female was about the same age as Skew Tusk but single-tusked. Rather like Inkosikazi, she seemed shy in her encounters with us. The last of the four was a rather striking cow who soon became my favourite. "Tatty Ear" was about 15 years of age, had small tusks and the most torn and tattered right ear imaginable. It was through Tatty Ear that I made my first breakthrough into being accepted by the herd.

We had been putting out salt at the mineral licks in the calcrete areas, particularly around Kanondo Pan, for about a year and would sit in a vehicle watching at some distance. Gradually we got closer and closer until we spread out the salt beside the vehicle in the hope that the elephants would come and siphon it up in their trunks.

It was the large looming shape of Tatty Ear one moonlit night that closed those last few spaces between us. My heart thumped with excitement as she slowly reached out her trunk to investigate the vehicle. In due course, she became more and more emboldened and would only give me a cursory examination before completely ignoring me. Her attitude had a calming effect on the other members of the family and soon the young males were joining in the nocturnal inspections.

During the second year, the elephants started drinking late in the afternoons. We would approach to within 250 metres of the group and switch off the engine. Any attempt to approach closer would sometimes send them scurrying off. This cautious behaviour on our part ultimately led to our complete acceptance by the herd and if we arrived at the waterhole before them they would come and drink or dig for minerals within 20 paces of us.

My first close contact during the day occurred one afternoon

'Inkosikasi' and 'Tatty Ear'

'Lodwa' and 'Skew Tusk'

These four were the senior cows
in the original herd when Alan Elliott first arrived
in 'Wankie'

David Shepherd

at Kanondo as the herd were scrambling close by for the salt which I had spread. Tatty Ear walked towards the vehicle and stood there towering above us. After viewing us for a few seconds she ambled off towards the waterhole closely followed by the whole herd which calmly walked past us as close as three metres. Only Skew Tusk looked unfriendly. What a great day! It had taken nearly two years of cautious persistence to reach this stage of familiarity.

Elephants obviously do have a great need for salt and I am certain it was our use of it in this way, more than anything, that helped to acclimatise them to the very close contact they have today with our vehicles and visitors. I became tempted, later on, to try to offer salt to the elephants from my hand to see what their reaction would be, but in this I was unsuccessful. The bolder young bull elephants would approach and put out a questioning trunk, but when they were less than a metre away, they would withdraw the trunk and shake it in a twisting action as though trying to throw off the disgusting human scent. They would then back-off a pace or two and stand and look at me, obviously craving the salt, but not quite

The vehicle is totally ignored as elephants search for salt.

ready to bridge that final gap.

At a later stage, I noticed that when the elephants had shaken down the Acacia pods, they would feed unconcernedly around the vehicle and then, again, the younger bulls, in their search for the pods, would place their trunks under the vehicle and if there was a pod there they would pluck it up. This led me eventually to carry pods in my vehicle.

I again attempted to see if that final barrier between elephants and man could be bridged by offering pods by hand and I have a very vivid memory of the first occasion in which

A game of 'Throw the Stick'.

an elephant came up and very, very gingerly, put out his trunk a few times before withdrawing quickly. Eventually, standing as far away from me as he could, but by straining forward, he plucked the first pod from my hand. It was a wonderful moment in which my feelings of intense elation were seasoned with a generous sprinkling of humility.

I had previously noticed that a particular elephant whom we later named Ndebele had always shown himself to be the most confident of the herd and the most curious about human beings. It was therefore no coincidence that he should have been the first to break that final barrier between us.

Although it is by far the most effective way in which wild animals can be programmed into accepting humans at touching distance, food as a stimulus should only ever be offered with a specific practical or scientific object in view. My initial aim was to build up the elephants' confidence in human beings which they never had before and I have been greatly rewarded to have experienced such a close relationship with these intelligent and sensitive animals. I regard many of them as my personal friends and I shall always treasure the memory of these early contacts.

I must, however, stress that feeding any wild animals can be extremely dangerous and should under no circumstances be attempted except under expert supervision. We have an absolutely strict policy of non-feeding of elephants by any of our staff. We do not allow elephants to approach nearer than three metres from our vehicles and all rangers are instructed to move away when elephants become too inquisitive. I have always been conscious of the danger of very close contact with even the most adaptable of our elephants. When you are very close to an elephant a sudden movement by an occupant of a vehicle could startle the animal, causing it to take a quick step back and perhaps throw up its trunk inadvertently. This action alone could cause very serious physical injury to anyone accidentally struck by the trunk.

Our policy now is to keep a reasonable distance from what are after all, free roaming, wild elephants. It is reward enough just to be able to sit close to them and observe them in their natural surroundings.

However, in the days when we were testing the reactions of the elephants and yearning to be accepted by them, I used to play games with the young bulls by lobbing sticks at their feet and they would often pick these up and flick them towards me in the vehicle and a sort of stick throwing game evolved. One day a young bull picking up a large dry stick near my

Landrover, walking up to the vehicle and banged his stick on the bonnet. Eventually, when he tired of his little game, he threw the toy away and wandered off.

The elephants and I invented another little game which became known as 'Throwing the Hat'. Originally I wanted to test the effect of human scent on the elephants by throwing my cap down in front of them when they came near my Landrover. Generally the cows would approach the hat with great reticence and stand some yards off. They would then reach out and immediately shake the trunk in an agitated manner, exhale and walk off ten or fifteen paces. However, some of the bulls would

The author getting acquainted with the elephants.

An elephant bull on the move.

pick up the hat and walk away with it. Others would chew it before dropping it. On one occasion I recall a bull picking up my hat, putting it in his mouth, walking off with it, dropping it and then, with his back foot, giving it a backward kick towards the vehicle!

I also found it essential to test the effect that human scent had on the elephants when we had gangs of men working on the Estate, repairing or building roads for example. Would it send the elephants scurrying off in a wild panic? In the very early days of Hwange Estate we certainly witnessed elephants stampeding from the traces of the scent of humans on the ground. Today it seems, in certain areas, especially at Kanondo Pan, the elephants are no longer greatly bothered by our presence as they have now come to accept the fact that humans are at work and represent no immediate threat. On the other hand, I have noticed that they are slightly more suspicious of the smell of man in areas further away from those habitually occupied by workers on the Hwange Estate.

The sight of humans out of a vehicle even at Kanondo still causes alarm to some of the elephants and this, as I have mentioned elsewhere, is one of the reasons why we do not walk around or carry out foot safaris any more.

A Charging Bull

Usually an alarmed elephant will run away. When the situation requires, it will put on a 'threat display' which may include a short 'mock charge'. Only under the most severe provocation in the defence of its young or if it is wounded or feels threatened will it actually charge. This can be most alarming but when the facts are examined afterwards, the elephant will almost always have a valid reason for its actions. I soon learnt that the best way to deal with a charging elephant when I was in a vehicle was to sit it out. Often the cows would charge at the Land Rover if they were surprised whilst trying to move away.

This posture is typical of an alarmed bull 'standing tall' doubtless in an effort to make himself look more impressive.

Right: Flapping of ears has nothing to do with aggression. Rather it allows radiated heat to escape the ear through the intricate blood vessel network. Blood returning to the body through the ear is several degrees cooler.

This bull elephant charging down
the road is probably a bull in
"musth". He can best be defferred
by revving the engine of the vehicle.

Left: An elephant comming forward
in a more liesurely manner.

In these circumstances, one or two of the large females would rush the vehicle with ears out, simultaneously letting off the most fearsome trumpet blasts. This was just a ploy to make room for the young to escape the perceived danger zone. If I sat still the mature cows would turn off and follow the retreating herd. Occasionally, a large bull would make a more determined approach and usually he could be stopped by revving the engine loudly. If all appeared lost, I also learned to become very aggressive, I would rev the engine and counter-charge. Unless there is a serious problem this is generally enough to make an elephant change its mind.

I have only had one serious experience of being charged by a bull. In 1977 I was driving down a narrow bush track with guests when I saw an elephant some 90 metres up the road. He was "standing tall" and slowly shaking his head from side to side. I foresaw trouble and brought the Land Rover to a halt 40 paces away. He bunched up, lowered his head and came down the road at great speed. I revved the engine as loudly as I could but he still came on. There was nothing for it but to engage first gear and charge him. Just before impact he lowered his head and the bumper made contact just above the base of his trunk. The vehicle bounced to the left and the elephant ended up on my right. With the elephant in hot pursuit, I just squeezed between two trees, made my way back onto the road and picked up speed. At this point, the elephant was only about five paces from the vehicle. I managed to accelerate back up to about 40 kph and slowly pulled away from the angry animal. After more than a kilometre he stopped pursuing us and I pulled up about 60 metres ahead. Anxious to see what the problem was, I stood on the seat and with my binoculars just had time to see bullet holes in his head, when he took up the chase again. Each time we got away I would stop, only to see him thunder down the track again. He finally gave up after more than four kilometres of pursuit. By this time we had been able to determine that he had been wounded several times in the face and head with a light calibre weapon.

The following afternoon I once again set out in the Land Rover when a spark plug malfunctioned. I would need to replace it that evening when I returned to base. In the meantime the vehicle had greatly reduced power. We were travelling along the Dete vlei road where the valley is at least 300 metres wide. My wife, Scotty, was the first to see an elephant running across the valley at full speed. We knew it must be the wounded bull and he made straight for the road ahead to cut us off. I did my best to coax the ailing vehicle to get to the meeting point first, but he was there waiting while I was 30 metres away. Down the road he came. I had no heart for another confrontation in my sick vehicle and veered off the road into the open valley. The downward slope assisted my speed and I finally managed to escape as his charge was not as persistent as on the previous day.

The matter was reported to the Department of National Parks. Their investigations led to a newly recruited ranger on patrol in the National Park who had wanted to try out an FN rifle to see if it could penetrate an elephant's head. He was dismissed the same day. I did not see that tortured bull again. He probably had left the Park for a quiet part of forest on the Hwange Estates. He would have been a formidable adversary had anyone come near him on foot and an unarmed person could easily have been killed. I trust that the bullets had passed through the skull and not through heavy flesh as this would have caused septicaemia and, almost certainly, death six to eight weeks later.

In the early and mid-seventies, it was our policy to conduct walking safaris. Of course, following a herd on foot is one of the best ways of getting to know the elephants. These safaris were very popular, as the number of tourists was low and we could spend a lot of time in the bush with our clients. In addition to following game we would impart bush lore and look at the botany and insect and bird life as well.

It is a most rewarding experience to see guests becoming proficient in reading the signs left along the trail. There are, in fact, numerous indications left by an animal as large as an elephant but despite this, they are not always easy to see and you can easily lose the "spoor" if you do not concentrate on what you are doing, especially if other animals have been criss-crossing a trail. It is quite usual inadvertently to confuse older spoor for the new and consequently go off on a wild goose chase. This does not matter greatly when I am alone, as there is immense enjoyment in tracking and 'reading' the activities of the herd. The problem arises when there are clients bent on taking photographs, whose only other wish is to catch up with the quarry as fast as possible.

Generally, it is easy to know how fresh the tracks are from their appearance. The fresher the track, the clearer and crisper the imprint. In the summer months tracks deteriorate much quicker. Wind, of course, makes tracks look older and you must take these factors into account. There are other aids to tracking. Sometimes you will be following what are clear imprints, with the elephants presumably close at hand, when the tiny prints of a mouse will be seen over the elephant spoor. Mice are nocturnal so if it is eight o'clock in the morning, the tracks are already a few hours old. Leaves knocked off branches dry out very quickly, especially in summer, and these also aid the tracker to estimate how soon he will catch up with the elephants. If there is a lot of litter to suggest the herd is feeding along slowly, then one can anticipate an earlier contact.

Elephant droppings contain a high degree of moisture and depending upon whether they have been deposited in the full sun or in the shade of a tree, their maturity can be assessed. Fresh dung is very warm and only becomes cold on the inside after 15 to 30 minutes. The tracker takes all these factors into consideration and this adds up to the fascination of the art. If the herd is moving with the wind, the elephants will detect the presence of the following human through his scent. It then becomes necessary for the tracker to move parallel with the tracks, say 100 metres to one side. Elephants, when feeding, can usually be heard from some distance. By occasionally

Fresh signs along the trail.

This ancient grove of *Acacia erioloba* has long been a favoured haunt of the elephants.

Opposite: Shade is vital for elephants, here a small family group share the sparse shade of an acacia tree.

checking the tracks and listening, the tracker can get ahead of the elephants and remain undetected.

I was always armed and I knew that my clients enjoyed the adventure of walking safaris and the element of tracking which went with it, but I felt that some people had unreasonably high expectations. I was often asked "can we get an elephant to charge?" I have always put the interests of wildlife first and naturally would never do anything to cause the animals distress. When one is in the company of five or six city dwellers who have not had an opportunity of developing bush sense, somebody can easily make a noise or move at a critical moment. Often after a successful track, we would be in a good position with the wind in our favour, and the herd moving steadily nearer as it fed and everybody hidden by trees or logs. Suddenly someone would decide to change position from one tree to another. This would immediately draw a response from the nearest elephant, who would throw up his head, spread his ears and 'stand tall'. Sometimes other elephants would be alerted by his gesture and become tense also. At other times, the alerted animal would follow his high posture with a short charge, trumpet and pull up just in front of the intimidated humans with a kick of sand from his forefoot. If he persisted

with his stance, I would have to bang two large sticks together and shout at him. He would then decamp very fast, taking the rest of the elephants with him in a retreat through the forest.

This was always a result I hated. In my view, a first rate safari guide should get his clients into a position to allow a good view, take some good photographs and make a quiet retreat. I always felt that I had done a satisfactory job when we achieved these results and the elephants never even knew that they had been observed.

Infrasound

I have thought for some years that there was, if you like, a kind of elephantine radio network or relay system in which crucial information could be rapidly communicated over a wide area between 'units' several kilometres apart. As I never heard any sounds, I was intrigued as to how the elephants achieved this. Since the recent discovery by the biologists Katharine Payne and William Langbauer that elephants can communicate through infrasound, some 15 different types of 'rumble', many of them inaudible to the human ear, have now been identified. Here are three examples of this extraordinary facility from my own experience.

I once noticed a bull elephant dozing under a large acacia tree. Upon my approach, he silently moved away. His companion, who had been lying down fast asleep some 50 metres away, immediately got to his feet and followed at a fast trot. On another occasion when I was out looking for elephants on foot with guests, we had taken a wide circular route without finding any sign of the animals. Suddenly there was the sound of trees crashing and a rumble, as a herd of elephants stampeded in our direction. They had obviously scented the fresh tracks of my party, stampeded in the opposite direction and straight onto us. Not wishing to be caught in the stampede, I hastily called to my clients to run with me to the safety of a

large fallen acacia tree lying in an open glade in the forest. We had just taken cover, when the front runners of the herd reached the glade. Picking up our scent again, they stopped in their tracks. Immediately there was total silence. I noticed some animals frozen with a foot off the ground. There was no movement and not a sound. After some thirty seconds, I leapt from behind the log and banged two sticks together, shouting at the same time. The animals crashed off again, making a great commotion. I estimated that there were 60 elephants in the group spread out over 75 metres and was amazed at the communication between all the animals and their instantaneous reaction to the command to stand still and maintain silence.

In 1988 our elephants disappeared overnight. Not one could be found for about ten days. They had moved away to the furthest reaches of the Sikumi Forest about as far away from Hwange National Park as they could go before moving into the communal area, which offers no safety at all. My investigations later revealed that on the day of their disappearance, a buffalo capture operation had begun 40 kilometres away in the Hwange National Park. This type of operation with heavy trucks moving into position, light aircraft overhead and helicopters buzzing around duplicates the activity of an elephant cull, but it would have been too distant to have been audible to the elephants in the normal way.

My friend Garth Thompson, who spent several years at the Hwange Estate and is now one of Zimbabwe's acknowledged experts on elephant behaviour, also observed a similar phenomenon on the Estate a few years earlier when an elephant cull was taking place in the Hwange National Park.

I have spent very many happy hours tracking elephants in the area and never cease to learn from these excursions. When tracking, you must always be listening ahead for the sound of elephants feeding, for the breaking of trees and so on. I remember on a walking safari about 15 years ago hearing the cracking of branches up ahead and confidently informing my group of guests that it was a herd of elephants feeding.

We approached carefully but all we found was a herd of eland, the largest African antelope the size of a large Brahman bull.

I was able later to observe a very large eland bull breaking branches from one of the trees by the action of placing its horns on either side of the bough and then twisting around until it fell to the ground, when the rest of the herd gathered around and fed on the leaves. From a distance, the sound was exactly the same as if the branches were being broken by feeding elephants.

Sometimes the elephants produce quite loud rumbles in their throats and this sound is of great help to the tracker in locating them. However, on three or four occasions now, I have been caught out by this sound. Recently while walking from my vehicle to inspect a water point I heard this low rumble. I stood for some considerable time looking in the direction of the noise, which was close by, but could not see any elephants. Only too late, did I realise that what I was hearing was the deep snarling of a lion, when three out of a party of four large male lions leapt up and loped away. The fourth animal lay growling for some time before standing up. By purposefully walking back to the vehicle, but at an oblique angle towards the lion,

After we accidentally walk into the four male lions, one turns to look at us.

I managed to make him move. He paused once to look back at me over his shoulder, then nonchalantly stalked away.

On another occasion, I remember hearing a rumble and, on turning around to suggest to the people following me that we should move around the wind as, again, I could not see the elephants, I saw through the corner of my eye some lion cubs running off. I immediately realised what the source of the noise was, and in that instant saw a mother lioness coming at great speed towards me. I was armed, as I normally am when I go in the bush, and presuming that the lioness was merely making room for her cubs to escape, I held my ground as she came charging up, emitting the most fearsome roars with every bound. I mentally drew a line demarcating what I considered to be my infringement zone and decided that if the lion persisted in her charge, I would reluctantly have to fire a shot either into the ground or at her. It was precisely at this point that she lay down and continued her snarling. Eventually, when she considered that she had made enough time for the cubs to get away, and urged on by my challenging shouts, she leapt up and trotted off in their direction.

I do not condemn the people who were standing behind me, who were totally unarmed, but when I turned around to judge their reaction, they were not there. It took me some time to find them hidden behind trees up to four or five hundred metres away. The first member of my party I came across was a young American cowering behind a large teak tree. "Wasn't that fantastic?", I said. "What was it?" he replied. "Lion," I said, "didn't you see it?." "No, I just noticed everybody taking off and when I saw the look in their eyes, I decided it was time to scoot as well!"

Lions have a great reputation for ferocity, but in my experience elephants are infinitely more formidable.

On another walking safari I had rather an unfortunate experience with an ostrich. An elephant herd I was following

had crossed the open Dete Vlei and I led my small party of safarists after them through the open valley. Halfway through the vlei, on looking some 200 metres to my left, I saw a male ostrich trotting towards me. Now, it so happens that I had introduced some ostrich chicks three years earlier onto the property as part of our game introduction programme. When these birds had reached sexual maturity they were released. Because they were hand reared and had lost their natural fear of man, during the breeding season, our males, unlike wild ostriches, could be very aggressive. I anticipated that we might have a problem, but thinking that the distance was too great, continued walking across the valley. This action seemed to spur the ostrich on, and it advanced at terrific speed towards us. As I had no cover whatsoever and there were no branches with which to fight the bird off, we stood our ground. He charged straight at me, thrust out his chest, sending me flying and, at the same time, started to kick me. Ostriches have strong muscular thighs muscles, designed to carry their heavy weight at great speed. It's toe has a large sharp claw which it uses for defence. With a characteristic slashing forward kick it ripped right through my clothing and made a deep cut on my stomach. I hung onto my rifle and rolled onto my side, whereupon the bird continued jumping up and down on me for what seemed like ages, but was probably only for 15 seconds or so. To my great relief the bird eventually stopped this silly action and I was still getting my wind back when I heard a scream. I looked up. The ostrich was now about to attack two of the lady members of my party.

I moved quickly to the side so that there would be no danger of inadvertently shooting my clients and fired a shot at where I thought the heart of the bird would be. This seemed to aggravate the ostrich which, once again, turned towards me. At this point I was in no mood to consider any humanitarian action and was about to fire again when the bird dropped dead at my feet. My guests and I barbecued him the next day!

It seems strange that in all the years that I have been tracking in the bush, this is the only injury which I have ever suffered.

As far as elephants are concerned, I have nearly always found it enough to shout at them or bang sticks together in an effort to deter them from any aggressive action. This method was used by Johnny Uys and, I am sure, by Africans for generations.

I have a vivid recollection one day of being out on safari and stalking a young bull elephant which presumably, on catching sight of one of the members of the party moving, decided to make a short rush at us. Concentrating on the animal and keeping a close eye on it, I commenced to bang a large stick against the base of a tree. This made a very impressive noise but did not seem to deter the animal. It was at this point that I heard a terrified yell coming from behind me. One of the ladies in the party lay on her back, holding her knee, screaming. I turned to look at the oncoming animal and, to my relief, saw that the noise must have deterred it, for it was making off at a fast trot with its head up, ears and tail out,

showing signs of alarm. In my effort to make a lot of noise I had broken my stick against the tree and a piece had flown back and hit the poor lady on the most sensitive part of her knee, causing her extreme pain.

Nowadays it is uncommon for a party of Germans to visit Hwange without at least one of the group being able to speak a smattering of English, but in the early 1970s, this was not the case and a group of half a dozen Germans came out on safari with me. We were walking towards one of the water holes at which there is a platform in the trees for observing game. I noticed that coming from a point slightly to our left and converging on the tree platform were about six very large elephant bulls. Encouraging my party to hurry, we ran towards the platform and just managed to climb up it without attracting the attention of the bulls which then started to drink and wallow.

There was also a lone warthog wallowing nearby which

A Blacksmith Plover alerts a bull elephant to her presence.

gave way for the bulls and stood some ten paces off, obviously awaiting their departure so that it could resume its wallow. After about five minutes of watching the large bulls I saw one of the ladies pointing to the warthog and murmuring something in a high pitched voice which sounded distinctly maternal. I was told afterwards by one of the party, through an interpreter, that she had mistaken the warthog for a baby elephant!

Many of the ground nesting birds appear to be at great risk when nesting near waterholes or along footpaths taken by elephants. I recall once seeing a Blacksmith Plover sitting on eggs at a very well patronised elephant mud wallow and I thought there would be little chance of this female rearing her young. In spite of my doubts, she successfully did so and I was fascinated to see how she defended her eggs when the elephants came down to the water. Being primarily a dark plumed bird the size of a pigeon, she would sit tightly on her eggs until an unsuspecting elephant walked nearby, whereupon she would let out a loud high-pitched screech and, at the same time, throw up her wings straight into the air, showing the undersides which are vividly white. This would be sufficient warning to the elephants who would step back and politely walk around the nest.

Inkosikasi flushes two kudu bulls from a mineral lick.

A bull checks out the scene before disturbing two sparring sable antelope bulls.

Crocodiles are treated with suspicion and are generally encouraged to return to the water.

Acacia erioloba pods: an important source of food in Hwange for many animals.

Right: Van Gogh (note his damaged ear!) shakes pods from an acacia tree.

Pod Collecting

Every one of the gnarled, old, flat-topped *Acacia erioloba* trees is linked to its neighbour by a maze of elephant paths trodden smooth by the grey giants as, like bees visiting all the blooms in a garden, they call on every tree to harvest the bounty. Competition is very fierce and by sitting quietly nearby one can observe the pecking order in operation. Only the most senior bulls are allowed a leisurely feed on the pods that have been shaken from the tree.

The method of shaking down the pods is very interesting to observe. The females seldom shake the trees, as this seems to be a predominantly male occupation. The bull will normally

feel out the tree very carefully and when he has found the best position, he will place the underside of his trunk along the main stem and then, with the deliberation of a professional golfer settling his feet into the sand, will hunch his back and give an almighty series of short shoves in quick succession which causes the tree to shake violently and rain pods down to the ground.

The sound of the falling pods invariably will cause other members of the group to leave their chosen trees and rush over to see what pickings they can get. Should the successful shaker be confronted by a more senior bull, he must give way or suffer the consequences of a tusk into his rib or backside. I have actually observed a large bull break off part of his tusk in this way. Of course, early in May there is an abundance of pods but, as the season wears on into late June, the harvest is drying up and competition becomes fierce. It seems that the cows are aware of the futility of attempting to compete in the feeding and only visit the acacia grove after the departure of the bulls in the hope of finding a few pods missed by the larger males. Procurement of food is often a case of opportunism and I have often observed families of cows and calves feeding very contentedly under the acacias, whilst in the canopy, wasteful Vervet monkeys or Chacma baboons are discarding half-eaten pods onto the animals below.

'Finger and thumb' delicately grasp a pod. Vervet monkeys are wasteful feeders of ripening acacia pods. On the ground below discarded pods are gratefully collected by cow elephants.

Wild Dogs

Cape hunting dogs are among the most feared predators in Africa. They are approximately the size of an Alsatian dog, but slighter in build. Their chief prey in Hwange appears to be the smaller antelope up to the size of female kudu and it is doubtful that they could take animals much larger than a zebra. I was therefore very intrigued recently, when I received a report from some of our rangers that they had sighted a small pack of five Cape hunting dogs surrounding a herd of elephant cows and calves on the Estate.

Immediately the dogs appeared on the scene, the elephants withdrew into a defensive circle, with the calves tucked in between them. Whenever one of the dogs approached too close to the herd, one of the female elephants would advance a short distance, trumpet at it, and return to the safety of her companions. Invariably the dogs would jump out of the way of the threatening elephant and then manoeuvre round to the other side to see if there were any easy pickings there.

I do not believe Cape hunting dogs are any threat to elephants. Perhaps, as is the case of all predators, they were simply probing the herd to see if there were any sick or injured calves amongst the group. The surveillance of the herd continued for some minutes, with the dogs occasionally seen to be standing on their hind legs in order to get a better view.

This, to my knowledge, is the only occasion on which such behaviour has been observed. Needless to say, after satisfying themselves that there was nothing to be gained by their continued observation of the elephants, the dogs jogged off to find easier prey.

It is surprising that the elephants formed a defensive circle, as on other occasions when I have seen lions in the vicinity, elephants have aggressively charged and driven them away.

Lion Drives

One of the most distinctive sounds on the Estate is the fury expressed by cows whenever they encounter lions. I have often witnessed well organised "lion drives", as the larger females form up in a battle line and sweep through the bush, heads held low, flattening every shrub to make sure that no lions are hiding there. These charges are characterised by a very high pitched, persistent and aggressive trumpeting, presumably reserved for the purpose of frightening lions out of the neighbourhood. Lions never attack fully grown elephants, but they are a potential danger to the very young. Abandoned or sick elephant calves are sometimes killed by lions. In a normal situation though, there is no chance of lions being able to kill baby elephants with their mothers present. Elephant mothers are fiercely protective of their young.

Man the Predator

The most formidable predator of all is, of course, man. After 20 years of gentle, protected treatment, the Presidential Elephants at Hwange have become among the most approachable in Africa. In my numerous encounters with the elephant herd I have had very many warming and emotional experiences, which when I have been sitting out in the bush I have had to remind myself that I have not been dreaming. It was one of those deliciously warm spring afternoons when 'David', named in honour of my artist friend, ambled over and eventually, tired of us and enjoying the warmth of the sun, crossed his legs and fell asleep on his feet, one of his tusks alongside my companion, Moffat Saunders. With a nod of approval from me, Moffat gently ran his hand along the tusk with a look of complete reverence on his face.

Mr Visitor Outcycles the Bull in Musth

Bulls in musth tend to be more aggressive than normal. We were sitting on the main road leading to Main Camp, watching a restless bull being a little bit aggressive. He would move back and forth between the trees and the road. So it was quite entertaining for the people in the vehicle when we heard this squeaking noise and turning round saw Mr Visitor on his bicycle making his way up the hill.

Mr Visitor was then a young man. He still runs the curio shop at the Hwange Safari Lodge and is a good friend of mine. I called across to him and said, "Watch out, this is an aggressive elephant." He laughed saying he was used to elephants, and with a shrug and a wave of his hand, started to ride past the animal at about 30 metres from it. This was when the elephant decided to go after him. Mr Visitor, who did not have much of a head start, began to pedal up the hill as fast as his legs could go.

An elephant in a hurry is faster than a horse and this one seemed to accelerate very quickly after the speeding cyclist. I started up my vehicle almost instantaneously and set off in hot pursuit. I managed to overtake a vehicle ahead of me and put my Landrover between the aggravated elephant and Mr Visitor. The elephant veered off into the bushes and we decided to ask Mr Visitor to describe his experience to us. We found him still pedalling hard, having travelled more than two kilometres in a remarkably brief space of time. We suggested to him that perhaps he should consider applying for inclusion in the Zimbabwe Olympic Cycle Team, but at that stage he was still too upset to see the joke!

Road signs carry a real warning. Elephants have a right of way.

100

Acute Sense of Smell

One morning, as I was leaving Sikumi Tree Lodge in my Landrover for the nearby Hwange Safari Lodge, I gave a lift to an African lady. Just before we reached our destination, we came across an elephant bull standing under an acacia tree.

I have always had an irresistible impulse to drive up to all the elephants I see and examine them. I therefore came off the road and stopped some twenty paces away from the animal. He immediately put up his trunk, seeming to sense that there was something he wanted in the vehicle. He approached at a steady pace. My poor passenger, who did not live in the area, was obviously petrified and decided to position herself on the floor of the vehicle. Much to her horror, the animal came right up to where she was crouching in the open Landrover and, reaching across her with his trunk, began to examine her property, which was contained in a small grass basket. Immediately aware of her anxiety, I drove off, but was curious to know why the elephant had taken such an interest in what I had thought to be her clothing. I was amused to learn that in a plastic packet beneath her clothes was a loaf of bread. I thought it remarkable that the elephant had smelt the bread at a distance of 40 paces particularly as, to my knowledge, bread is unknown to members of the Presidential Herd of Elephants.

An elephant bull inquisitively approaches the vehicle.

A tranquil scene in
front of the Hwange
Safari Lodge.

Skew Tusk meets David Shepherd

Unlike the bread-loving bull, Skew Tusk has always tended to be slightly aggressive. She certainly does not like vehicles to be driven too close to her and she will not tolerate them being driven through the bush when she is feeding. I recall the first visit to Hwange Estates by David Shepherd, the eminent wildlife artist and superb painter of elephant.

I offered to show him elephants shortly after his aircraft had landed late that afternoon, but I just could not find them and with David that is a disaster. Feeling very determined to prove that we really did have the best, friendliest elephants in the world, I finally came across Skew Tusk feeding about 40 metres off a track in thick bush.

Against my better judgement, I steered the vehicle into an impossible position in the thick bush. Just when I could not manoeuvre the vehicle in any direction, Skew Tusk let out the bellow that she reserves for such occasions and bore down on us with her high-stepping gait and ears drumming against her shoulders to make the maximum noise, sending sticks and branches flying. I relied on my only defence by being counter-intimidatory and revved the Land Rover as hard as I could. It worked and she stopped short of us. David was on the side the elephant came from, so that I could see his face as I was watching Skew Tusk's progress. I now know what a man looks like when he thinks he is going to die! David was not impressed with me. We had only met an hour before and he admits to having had very serious doubts about his guide. What bad luck for me that our only elephant on the first day had to be Skew Tusk in thick bush!

A Lucky Escape

I was driving down back to my house at about ten o'clock in the evening, when a man ran into the road without a shirt on and in an obviously emotional state. He was jabbering and I presumed that he was drunk, which as he had been near the local railway siding, was not so unusual. It took me a little time to realise he was begging me for a lift. So as it was late at night I took him to my home.

He was bleeding quite badly all over his body, and I asked the staff to look after him. I said he was drunk and in the morning they should send him on his way. However, the next day my staff told me the man had not been drunk at all. In fact they had sat until the early hours of the morning, pulling hundreds of thorns out of his body, the result of his having been chased into some thickets of thorns by an enraged elephant.

He had only just escaped being killed. About two hours after we had sent the man on his way, the police arrived and asked me if I would mind escorting them into the nearby bush to search for a man who had been killed the previous day by an elephant. It did not take very long to realise that they were talking about the same man and I asked how they knew he had been killed. They told me that he and his co-workers had been loading some timber at the railway siding. They were waiting for transport to take them home, when they were engaged by an elephant. They scattered in all directions and saw the elephant bull about to crush the man. Presuming him dead they made a report to that effect. It was the same man who had had a narrow escape.

Introducing Babies

Ridge is one elephant that has become particularly accustomed
to us; she is totally confident and when she approaches us, she is
so relaxed that she allows her calves to accompany her.
Furthermore, you would expect that if she were the slightest
suspicious or nervous she would act as many other animals do,
shielding the baby by placing it on the far side of herself. By
contrast, she will walk around the vehicle looking for pods,
allowing her baby freedom to go where it wants. This is a result
of never being harassed in any way.

Mothers bring their babies to us quite routinely now, but
I do recall a specific incident when I was making a film for one
of the British television companies. There were about 40
elephants milling around collecting mineral salts at a salt lick.
We had been there for about 15 minutes when a cow came out
of the bush right up to my vehicle door with a baby to which she
had given birth within the last hour. It was less than a metre high
and had pink ears and blue eyes. The cow stood by and guided
her baby with her trunk as it came up with wobbly legs to the
vehicle. They stood there for a couple of minutes and then
walked off. Millions of TV viewers were able to witness the
event.

I felt in that moment that we had gained total and complete
acceptance as part of the herd for that young mother to have
done this. It was a high point in our relationship with the
Hwange Estate elephants.

That cow elephant has extremely jagged ears. She should be
very well known, but I have not seen her since, to my
knowledge. Yet, she had to be one of the Presidential Elephants,
because an elephant unfamiliar with the Estate would not have
acted in that way.

**A contented elephant
calf suckles from its
relaxed mother.**

104

Playful Young Bulls

Young bulls are quite playful and like giving chase. Often at the borehole pans you will see a young bull chasing doves or guinea fowl or some little animal, even kudu. This behaviour starts off as a casual game, frequently developing into an irresistible impulse to follow and have more fun. Should the 'victim' run away, the bull will keep pursuing it. When anything larger stands its ground, the elephant will veer off with a kick of its foot.

We have never even had a vehicle dented. The young bulls will come up and play with the aerial and recently one put its foot on the bumpers as if to say, "you can't go any further". They like to play with the vehicles and I think they realise there is no danger. It is an amusing way of trying out their strength, so when I am alone I just put the car into neutral and let them push me down the road. Sometimes I play ' bull pushing', in the same way that two young bulls will push against each other. This is when I might reverse up against a youngster just to play with him. They seem to enjoy it and it does them no harm.

I have been asked whether I think the elephants are in danger of becoming too friendly. We have to recognise that there is a point at which you cease the familiarity. I believe we may have reached that stage now bearing in mind these are wild animals.

Bulls to the Rescue

A remarkable example of lack of compassion for "strange" calves occurred a few years back, but with a surprising twist. Bryn Jolliffe, my Senior Ranger, radioed in late one evening to report that a one day old calf had fallen into the two metre deep ditch dug around the Hwange Safari Lodge to prevent elephants straying into the Lodge grounds. Bryn wondered what to do. I had no doubt that the right thing was to place the little creature near the waterhole some fifty metres away. I reasoned that if its mother was dead, hyenas would kill it, or, if the mother was inexperienced and somehow lost the calf, she might find it. I did not imagine that the mother of so young a calf could easily lose it, and I feared the worst.

I should state here that although I have heard it being done by an elephant expert in Kenya, in Hwange it has so far proved impossible to rear an unweaned elephant calf. Bryn felt too much compassion to accept my decision and took the calf in a Land Rover to reunite it with a herd known to be feeding a few kilometres away. By the time he found the herd, the little calf was screaming blue murder and with a rumble the elephants rushed up to inspect the source of the noise. The rangers hastily put the calf down and drove away. The sun had set and it became too dark to study events after that.

The following evening, as a breeding herd of cows and calves were bathing and being observed by some of our guests, three large bulls walked down the acacia lined slope with the newborn abandoned calf at foot. One of the bulls then walked the calf up to a cow and induced it to try and suckle. The latter presented her rear end to the calf and then, with a vicious kick, sent it flying. Enraged, one of the other concerned bulls rushed up and tusked the cow in the ribs. She let out a yell of agony and ran off, closely followed by the rest of the breeding group. Within half an hour, another group of cows and calves arrived at the waterhole and the episode was re-enacted exactly as before.

The three bulls then walked the tiny calf into the water and it made valiant efforts to gulp some liquid down. With the sun setting, the three bulls turned and walked up the slope, closely followed by the weak-legged baby. Soon the slow lumbering giants and their little orphan were enveloped in the blackness of the forest. The following day a ranger, reacting to the site of vultures gliding from the heavens, came across the remains of a young female elephant. She had died giving birth.

Over the next few days some of my younger and less experienced rangers reported that they had seen the calf. Some said that it was seen suckling, others that it had been adopted. Their hearts were ruling their eyes. That is not Nature's way. We never did see that calf again. However, I was astounded by the generous behaviour of the kindly bulls.

At a crowded waterhole, an elephant bull accidentally knocks over a small bull. Instantly the protective mother moves in.
A mother expertly lifts her calf from a mud hole.

Inkosikasi Rescues a Toddler

One evening I heard an awful screaming and trumpeting near Lodge pan. The sounds told me that there was a problem, and I rushed down to investigate. A toddler had fallen into the cement trough and was too small to climb out on its own.

Just as you would expect in a human situation, the mother and all the young aunts were running around screaming. Now and again one of the adults would have a look at the struggling calf and run off trumpeting. Occasionally a larger animal would get on its knees and try to lift out the infant; sometimes two or three would be trying at one time. It was a scene of chaos and confusion. At last the large, recognisable shape of Inkosikasi could be seen striding purposefully back from the acacia forest. Pushing the panicking aunties away, she calmly knelt down and bodily lifted the calf from the trough with her trunk. She has no tusks and so could not use them as a fork lift as tusked animals can. She knew what she had to do and in a quiet, dignified manner succeeded at the first attempt. Once the calf was on firm ground, the anxious mother rushed forward and, like a woman hugging her child in a similar situation, moved off quickly with her trunk holding the little calf against her body. After a little more trumpeting and a lot of deep lion-like roars, the family departed into the silence of the forest.

I have seen similar situations on many occasions and the similarity to human behaviour in times of disaster is unmistakable. However there are important differences. Once a calf has been "imprinted" upon its mother at birth, an intimate and permanent bond is forged. Should a cow lose her calf and another calf lose its mother, the cow will not adopt. Unlike other animals, cows will only suckle their own calves.

The trunk of an
elephant is really an
extension of the
upper lip and nose.

Mercy Killing

It is always sad to learn of the death of one of the elephants. It is traumatic when I have to shoot an animal that is injured beyond hope and is suffering. Normally I draw the line between man-inflicted injury and an ailment brought about naturally. In the latter case I tend to let nature take its course. Seriously injured elephants tend to find comfort in packing their wounds with mud or by standing for hours on end in the water and sometimes they do recover.

On one occasion I had to put a young animal out of its misery when it was hit by a train. The left foreleg was shattered with large splinters of bone sticking out at different angles. The difficulty of moving with only one front leg can be imagined and yet this poor animal hobbled and stumbled a distance of five kilometres from the site of the accident.

On another occasion I was called to inspect a very ill animal. It was one of our friendly bulls. A glance at the wretched animal standing in the pool was all that was necessary to see that he had been wounded by gunfire. He was blind in one eye, had chips out of one tusk and had the tell-tale bleeding holes. The area around the wounds was very swollen and pus was leaking out. He was just skin and bone. One bullet from a .370 rifle through the brain brought instantaneous relief. When we inspected his body we discovered ten bullet wounds from FN rifles and two heavy calibre bullets. The shooting had been indiscriminate, mainly in his rump and stomach. Gallons of pus gushed from the wounds when they were opened. Severe septicaemia had set in and the poor animal must have suffered indescribable pain. Bullets from an FN rifle or a .375 magnum sprayed into non-vital areas of the body cannot immediately kill an elephant. Whoever shot this animal knew that. They were just having fun! I shudder when I think of the poor beast running across an open area with the fearful crack of rifle fire behind. I envisage the dust flying off his hide, the flinching with pain as each bullet drove deeply into his flesh...and the grinning idiots behind the rifles. It would have taken six weeks for the septicaemia to set in and bring him to death's door. What do you do with people who behave in such a barbaric manner? I suppose you can only try and educate them.

Several of the bull elephants have lost their lives as a result of accidents, however I do not remember any of the cows dying as the result of a mishap. A fairly common cause of accidental death anywhere, results from the animals becoming stuck in the mud whilst wallowing. This usually occurs during the hot, dry months of September or October and an agonising death from thirst and exposure follows if they are not shot. Whenever smaller elephants are stuck, they can be rescued by removing some of the mud and pulling them out with stout ropes behind a tractor. This is hazardous work as the poor animals mistake our

good intentions and lash out with their trunks.

One large bull showed signs of extreme distress and hobbled along, hardly able to put one of his forefeet down. Eventually he would stand around for most of the day in a waterhole. After 14 days, when it was apparent that he was in great pain, he was shot. The cause of his problem was nothing more than a piece of wood about one inch thick and six inches long which had lodged in the foot causing septicaemia. It was very surprising that such a seemingly minor injury could have been so devastating.

A Double Tragedy

A very tragic accident occurred one evening, when a vehicle being driven by one of the local policemen from Dete station drove at great speed into the side of an elephant. Elephants can be very hard to see at night and when confused by the dazzling lights do not always move off in the right direction. The impact of the vehicle on this occasion stove the ribs of the elephant into his lungs and he died on the spot. Unfortunately, the young man was also killed outright.

Mud bathing by the more adventurous young bulls sometimes leads to tragedy. The animals can get stuck in the deep mud and often are unable to escape.

This elephant saw the train approaching from a long way off, but still decided at the last moment to cross in front of it! Occasionally elephants are killed in this way.

Right: The agony of this snared Hyena can only be imagined. Ultimately death is merciful.

Damaged Trunk

One of the bulls on the Estate, when I arrived there, had a very short trunk. What was left of it was about 12 inches long and very pink on the end, showing two gaping nostrils. We all presumed that the trunk had been caught in a snare and had rotted off. Snares are set by subsistence poachers, usually with the intention of catching animals up to the size of buffalo, but definitely not elephants. The snare is usually made of steel cable and consists of a running noose. As the end away from the noose is tied tightly to the bough of a tree, the animal cannot escape. When it puts it head through the cunningly concealed loop and moves forward, the noose tightens around the neck. The more the panic stricken animal pulls against the snare, the tighter it becomes until the victim is strangled.

Sometimes an elephant gets its trunk caught in the noose but, because of its great strength, can usually break the bough from the tree. By this time, the noose is so tightly wrapped around the trunk that it cuts very deeply into the flesh. As the elephant moves off dragging the bough the noose is tightened even further whenever it gets snagged up on trees or fallen logs and it is necessary for the ensnared animal to wrestle itself free. This action and festering of the wound eventually causes the cable to work its way through the flesh until the trunk falls off and frees the elephant from its agony. Of course the elephant, being very dependent on its trunk for both feeding and drinking, would have suffered severe disability whilst ensnared. Once the trunk has fallen off, the elephant must learn to readjust to its severe disability. Drinking creates a massive problem and the poor animal must either get onto its knees to drink or else wade chest deep into the ponds. Equally, feeding becomes very difficult

because an elephant has an extremely short neck and depends upon its trunk, not only for putting food into its mouth but also to identify by smell what it is about to eat.

Additionally, a trunk has many other uses, including a wonderful "finger and thumb" on the end, which it uses delicately to pluck objects such as leaves or to gather pods. The particular elephant I have mentioned, became very skilled at feeding. He developed a technique for gathering roots, branches and grass by scraping his feet. He would then carefully balance the food on his right foot and slowly lift it up to his trunk stump. From there he could transport it to his mouth. Because of the constant bending forward he developed huge neck muscles the size of a football and this made him look hunchbacked. However, he persisted and flourished.

One day, information was passed on to me that an elephant had been struck by a train and killed. I hastened to the scene and was met by the gory sight of fifty or more local people engaged in the business of butchering the carcass. As the body had already been dismembered, I hastily enquired after the tusks and ears as these can facilitate identification, but before they were produced, I noticed the trunk still attached to the skull. It was only a foot long and had two gaping nostrils. By coincidence, I subsequently heard from a railway train driver, who said that he had once accidentally knocked down an elephant near the same spot some years previously. The elephant fell clear but the trunk was lying across the rails and most of it was severed. It now seems that our unfortunate elephant lost his trunk not from a snare, but a train. What an irony that after surviving the first accident, he should have died under the wheels of another steam train.

Death in the Forest

On a warm summer's day in February 1981, I set out in the Landrover with an eager party of visitors. We headed down the Dete valley in the direction of Kanondo.

On reaching the waterhole, I was happy to see two or three large bulls standing there. I approached them in my usual slow manner and was delighted to see my old friend "Tatty Ear" and her young two year old son, Henry. After a short while, I realised that there were no other females or calves around. This is most unusual and the only conclusion to be drawn was that the female herd had moved along, leaving "Tatty" in the company of suitors. Her calf was of an age when he would be weaned and, presumably, his mother was again coming into oestrus. This would explain the presence of the large bulls.

We watched the little group for some time, but no mating took place, so we drove off into woodland and decided to leave the vehicle in order to lead my guests on a short walk.

The Bush at this time of the year is at its densest, being heavily leafed, in addition to which, the grass is lush, green and, in places, waist high. Visibility is reduced to between 15 and 30 metres in this type of woodland, but in some places can be as little as five metres. We had been walking from the vehicle for no more than 10 minutes when I came across fresh signs indicating that an elephant herd had passed by within the preceding 30 minutes. Cautioning my party to follow in single file and in silence, I immediately took up the spoor.

After a few minutes, I noticed some 10 metres away to my right a bundle of grass which had been chewed and spat out. I held up my hand to indicate to the party to stand still and squatted down in the silence of the forest to inspect the rejected food. I was still engrossed in my study when one member of the group of people said quite calmly, "There is an elephant coming up behind us". I sprang to my feet, turned around, and saw a large grey shape bearing down upon us at great speed. Visibility was not good and my impression was mainly of trees being bent over as only occasionally did I get the briefest view of the elephant's outline. From where I stood, I calculated that the animal was headed on a line some six or seven paces to my right and straight at my clients. To turn an elephant in these circumstances it is usually sufficient to shout very loudly and this is what I did. The result on this occasion, however, was to cause the animal to change its course and veer straight towards me. A safari guide in these situations must react speedily and correctly. Emotions must be cast aside and the safety of guests given urgent priority. It was then that I raised my .458 rifle, followed the animal's head through the bushes and fired.

Instinctively, I knew that I had not made the brain shot I had intended. I quickly I reloaded and fired at the only clear target I could see above the bush in front of me. As the animal's head was now very low, I had to shoot over the neck and into the spine. With a skidding crash the elephant fell at my feet and, for the first time, I noticed a calf standing alongside its fallen mother. I turned to check on my clients who were all bunched together right at my shoulder. Slowly I moved forward and saw to my absolute horror a tattered and torn ear, limp against the large skull. It was Tatty Ear.

After a lapse of about 15 minutes, two bull elephants arrived on the scene and, with trunks outstretched, smelled her vulva. One of the males then straddled her body and attempted a mounting but finding this impossible tried to lift her from the ground. The other male then joined in but their attempts were in vain, and they eventually retired. Henry all this time remained near his mother's body and steadfastly refused to allow us to approach. In great sadness I returned to the vehicle. If tracking elephants could lead to this type of tragedy, then I reasoned it was not worth the price. I have never led another walking safari on the Hwange Estates. The following morning, when I returned to the site of the previous day's tragedy, Henry had gone. I saw him two days later with the breeding herd and as he had been weaned, I presume that he has survived. With hindsight I can now speculate that Tatty was not charging us but, having dallied with the bulls at the waterhole, was running to catch up with her family and, finding us in her path, became confused. Had she known exactly where we were, I now feel that she would probably have avoided us. My anguish is even greater.

David Shepherd

Listening Quietly at Night

Sit very quietly when you are in the bush. You have to use all of your senses. You must look and observe. You must hear and you must use your sense of smell. You must learn to reach out to Nature. It is a total sense experience. Often I will go out at night with people and sit with elephants or lions. I will switch off the engine and sit with straining eyes in the pitch darkness. It is always a rewarding experience because my guests are sharp and alert. They are listening for every little sound. They are using their noses and that is a very important part of being in the bush, feeling that empathy. It is very hard to achieve this when you are with a lot of people. You realise when you are a professional guide, that people understandably want to see things and take photographs. Until they have been to Africa a few times, many people are simply not ready to want to experience listening, smelling and feeling the atmosphere around them just for the sake of it. To appreciate it to the full, you have to be out at night under the glittering darkness of an African star-filled sky.

Male Puberty

Elephant herds are matriarchal. When the young males reach puberty, which in Hwange is between about 12 and 14 years of age, they are evicted by the females. This is a particularly emotional experience for the animals concerned, as they are constantly attacked and are made to feel generally unwanted. After a period of three to six weeks of following in the wake of the herd, they attach themselves to a group of bulls. These groups are termed "bachelor herds" and are a useful stepping stone into the all-male world, with its new set of social intricacies. It seems that the young males move around between individual groups, before settling into a more permanent bond of companionship. It is too early to know with how many groups a male will associate until he settles into a permanent

A young elephant feeding at night.

male group. Sometimes a teenager will attach himself respectfully to a single, more senior bull. In this role he is known as an 'askari'. A human equivalent might be an apprentice or a body guard.

It is not certain if there is ever anything permanent, or what would break up a male bond grouping. We plan to make this the basis of a long-term study. On the Hwange Estate, the size of male groups vary between two and 25, with five or six

Right: Adolescent elephant bulls enjoy the physical contact that comes from being part of a 'Bachelor Group'.

apparently being a usual number. Our most recognisable duo is a youngish bull with a dreadfully mangled ear, appropriately named Van Gogh, and his companion, Rembrandt. These two will be closely watched in order to fill in some of the missing pieces of information.

The Whinger

Population reduction exercises carried out within Hwange National Park aim at eliminating whole families in order to minimise emotional distress. Inevitably in operations so difficult, occasionally, there is the odd survivor. One young male elephant arrived and took up residence on the Estate. To all intents and purposes he appeared to have been one such survivor. However, no culling operations have been carried out for some years. So where did he come from and why? This particular animal is about 10 years of age and probably too young to have been evicted from his family herd, as is the case with all post-pubertal males. For over a year, this lonely young animal has wandered around the Estate alone. He cuts a pathetic little figure as he goes around all day, talking to himself through a series of squeaks and moans and, often, with the tip of his trunk in his mouth for comfort almost like a baby's dummy. The interesting thing is that even now, he has still not been accepted by any of the other males. I presume, when he reaches puberty, that he will be allowed to join the club, but it is an interesting situation. One unkind ranger dubbed him "the Whinger" and the name has stuck.

Pseudo Sexual Behaviour

Many observers have seen the pseudo sexual behaviour carried out by young elephants, mainly through the mounting exercise. Quite often, elephants of only a year or less are observed to do this and it is quite common to see post pubertal bulls in the 15-20 age group mounting. I have always taken this to be a sign of dominance, that is the dominant animal mounting a subservient animal, merely to prove a point. I have never really thought that there was any adolescent sexual implication in this act until, very recently, when I was sitting at Red Pan, near Ivory Lodge, one rainy afternoon amongst a very large and playful group of elephants. Two young males close to the vehicle went through this pseudo sexual act and I was most surprised to see the dominant male ejaculating, until streams of sperm were running down the legs of the sub-dominant animal. There was no question of any penetration, but the ejaculation was clearly the result of sexual excitement.

Another fairly common occurrence is to see young bulls using their trunks to smell the genital area of other elephants and, again, this seems to be another aspect of adolescent sexual experimentation.

Covering up after Birth

I came along a forest track late one evening and found a large group of elephants, very reluctant to move off the road. A cow had just given birth to a calf. She defecated and all her family came around and ate the dung. I had never observed this before, but this behaviour suggests that the dung may contain some tell tale scent which could inform a potential predator that a calf has been produced. This would link in with the devouring or burying of the foetal sac membrane by elephants.

Attitude to Vehicles

Elephants show no concern for humans in a vehicle, but become distinctly nervous at the sight of the upright ape. Man has been a serious predator for so long that the fear and mistrust is deeply ingrained. Vehicles are very recent arrivals and unless used regularly for hunting, do not appear to be retained in the memory as dangerous. We have always been most careful never to give the elephants any reason to resent us in our vehicles.

chin rubbing

Rock Hyrax
Procavia capen
Africa. SW Asia.

120

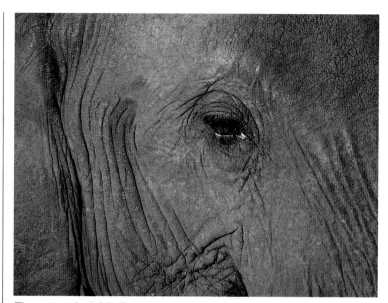 

The eye on the left indicates an elephant at ease; that on the right, stress.

For example, we will not follow the animals if it appears to us that they wish to move way or that they are simply tired of us being around. This acclimatisation of elephants does go beyond vehicles and despite what I have said already, there are certain areas where elephants do tolerate humans walking around.

Boundaries

They appear to know the boundaries of photographic safari camps within sanctuaries and will move around freely in search of pods or water in the dry season, despite humans walking close by. In some areas, the bulls become pests and will help themselves to fruit from vehicles or tents. Away from these camps, the elephants are not as tolerant of humans. I consider the elephant to be potentially the most dangerous African animal, to be approached on foot with the utmost care. Normally elephants will move away, but if ever they feel threatened, particularly if they have young, they are capable of

great aggression. For this reason, we do not approach the elephants on foot. We have no wish to disturb them or ever to have to kill an animal in "self defence" again, as was the case with Tatty Ear. By understanding the rules and abiding by them, we have never had a single incident where anybody has been placed in jeopardy in thousands of encounters.

Elephants soon learn the boundaries of safety and if it becomes necessary or desirable to leave sanctuary areas, they generally move out at night. It is well known that whenever elephants leave the National Park to raid gardens in the adjacent communal areas, they will muster near the boundary at sundown, move across the borderline in the early evening and, after a hearty feed, will re-cross into the safety of the Park at about 4:00 am. Similarly, the Estate elephants, if they do leave for visits to neighbouring farms, will do so at night. It is the responsibility of the bulls to reconnoitre the ground. Only after the area is thought to be safe, will the female herds follow.

Kanondo

Kanondo waterhole is probably one of the best places in the world to study elephants. Apart from the mineral licks, there is an ample supply of pumped water both for drinking and bathing purposes. Elephants are passionately fond of fresh, clean water and will travel many miles, often passing stagnant pools, in order to reach it. For this reason we have also constructed concrete ponds on the Estate into which clean water is pumped.

When elephants are under no stress they will not go very far from water, and the Presidential Elephants tend to operate between pumped waterholes. They may drink at a source one day or for up to six days in a row. Then for a change, they will go the following evening and drink at one of the other waterholes, five or six kilometres away at most. The elephants here tend not to travel much more than eight kilometres in a day, but obviously are quite capable of covering vast distances in districts where they are hunted or where they go crop raiding before returning to sanctuary areas.

As we have no natural sources of permanent water such as rivers on the Estate, it might be said that by installing waterholes we are getting away from the idea of a totally natural environment. We do pump water, but the alternative is really unthinkable, that is to pump no water at all and have the elephants wander into areas where, perhaps, they might be shot by other people, or where they would cause a nuisance to the neighbouring folk in the communal areas.

The bulk of the elephants tend to stay close to home. It is possibly the safest place for elephants in Zimbabwe. True, they will move into the Hwange National Park, where water is also pumped and into the adjoining forest area, but will not wander far away. Certain individuals, like Disc, the one with the floppy ear, disappears for several months at a time and Carrot and a few other characters come and go. It is significant that we have

**Anyone at home?",
the elephants seem to
be saying as they
check out the
underground hide at
Kanondo for human
occupants.**

**Right: Glossy Starling
and Crimson Breasted
Shrike.**

no recorded sightings of known elephants more than 30 kilometres from the centre of the Estate. Perhaps some individual males may move greater distances but most, even our dominant elephant bulls seem to prefer to stay close at hand and, certainly, the main breeding cow herds show no intention of emigrating.

Our visitors are always surprised to learn of the elephants themselves playing a considerable role in the making of the waterholes. Originally they would have come to an area such as Kanondo for the mineral salts. They would have excavated and devoured tons of soil and ended up with a wide, shallow

depression. Over the centuries, they would have dropped sticks and grass and dung. Eventually, in the process of 'puddling' by the elephants, an impermeable seep-proof clay layer would have formed and this would have held water when the rains came and provided a reserve of water at the beginning of the dry season, until it was time to head for the rivers.

By installing pumped water at Kanondo, we have provided an essential all the year round facility both for our animals and the guests who come to see them.

A bird much in evidence around the elephants at Kanondo is the Yellow Billed Hornbill. He spends his time usefully opening up drying elephant dung for the termites it contains. The Hwange National Park boasts over 400 species of bird and the Estate is equally blessed. Among the most brilliant birds to be found around the water holes, are the irridescently blue, Glossy Starlings and the bustling Crimson Breasted Shrikes.

Butterflies, too, are often in evidence where elephants have been. The yellow Corps de Ballet and Charaxes, fluttering in orange, white and blue, both find the dung a useful source of food and moisture.

Jan Teede, who took the picture of the toad lurking in a large pile of elephant dung, had never seen this phenomenon until his wife, Fiona, pointed out a somewhat thwarted Spotted Bush snake wondering where his next meal had disappeared to!

Termites

Termite mounds are to be found on the Estate, where there is clay. They form part of the intricate web in the ecosystem. The termites take the dung deep into the soil, partly as nutrient for themselves because their digestive system is capable of breaking down the cellulose and partly to provide manure for their fungus gardens deep in the ground. They create elaborate thermo regulatory systems in the form of chimneys and ducts to allow for ventilation.

After only six months, the elephant dung has been completely broken down and the soil has been improved. The termites themselves also play a dynamic role in the complex chain of existence at Hwange. For the elephants they supply minerals, which they bring up to the surface and their tall mud edifices often provide useful scratching posts. They unwittingly act as hosts for seeds defecated by birds and play a vital part in the germination of the Ebony Tree, the seeds of which grow on termite mounds after having been defecated by baboons on sentry duty. The nocturnal Aardvark, in his pursuit of termites for food, uses his sharp claws to excavate tunnels in the mounds. In due course, these become holes for porcupines and warthogs and, when enlarged, for Hyenas. Mongooses live and breed in the hollows of the ventilation shafts and bees build their hives in chambers in the mounds.

This toad escaped from a snake by hiding in elephant dung.

Right: A Yellow Billed Hornbill hunts for termites in elephant dung.

The calm eye and relaxed position of the ears indicates an elephant at ease, despite the close proximity of the photographer.

Managing Elephants

Emotionally I am extremely uncomfortable about the possibility of elephant culling being renewed in Zimbabwe, and in the Hwange National Park in particular. I admit, as a former hunter, who carries a full Ranger's Licence, that I am now somewhat biased against the killing of all game. I realise that there are arguments made by many distinguished scientists in favour of culling, which command considerable respect, but as a bush man, with no scientific background, I can perhaps offer some of my own observations, which may add something useful to the debate.

Rising Elephant Population

The simple answer given to the question, "Why do we cull?" is "Because we have too many elephants". Unlike most other African countries, Zimbabwe has an excellent record for its management of wildlife. In Africa as a whole, the elephant population has fallen drastically over the last ten years - from 1.3 million to 600,000. The depredation of poaching cartels attempting to satisfy the demands of the international ivory market is, as most people agree, the principle cause, but growing human population pressures on wildlife habitats have also been an important secondary factor. In Zimbabwe, our elephant population continues to expand. Estimates vary between 50-70,000. For the last ten years, aerial surveys have been used to count the numbers of elephants in different types of habitat. I have been told that the surveys for Hwange have proved quite consistent and that overall, our elephant population is increasing at a rate of between 3-5% per annum. In demographic terms, this would be considered a population explosion. The elephant's only predator is man. In the 1960's the public were pleased to see the growth of the elephant population since, in the last century, so many had been slaughtered for ivory; but in the 1970s people began to notice the damage in the Hwange National Park around some

A large group of elephants come for a mid-day drink at Mpofu pan on the Hwange Estate.

waterholes where vegetation appeared to be significantly affected, sometimes up to a kilometre beyond a pan.

In certain places in Zimbabwe, in the Zambezi Valley for example, at Chizarira, the riparian damage is very noticeable. A restricted environment where the elephants are presently annihilating their own habitat, it may be correct to suggest that this type of setting should only support an elephant population of between 0.2 and 0.7 elephants per square kilometre. Nevertheless the core of my argument is that what may accurately apply to one area, does not necessarily pertain to another. What is important, is that all the parameters should be identified and subjected to individual analysis before any irrevocable decisions are made.

On the Hwange Estate, we have a range of vegetation and a savannah type of woodland which, although it may be vulnerable to fire and frost, is able to support a high elephant population as well as a balanced proportion of other wildlife, without detriment to the vegetation. There has, in fact, never been a full-scale measurement of the vegetation nor the overall changes that take place in the vegetation in our area, nor in its capacity to sustain a balanced, mixed mammal 'economy'. As elephants are known to eat more than 150 types of plant, I am anxious that long-term decisions on our elephant population should not be made without as much information as possible being made available. National Parks estimate present elephant numbers in the Hwange National Park to be 26,500. It is proposed that the correct elephant population there should be in the order of 13,000.

Effective Rainfall but False Conclusions

The rationale of the present thinking is based on studies in the 1970s, which suggest that there is a linear relationship between rainfall and large herbivore biomass - including other large herbivores in addition to elephants. The scientists estimate the numbers of all the animals in an area and suggest that there should be a certain balance between elephants and the other herbivores. The amount of rainfall is then taken into account. It is postulated that Hwange's 600mm of annual rainfall should allow the Park no more than 13,000 elephants, or approximately one of these animals per square kilometre.

There are conflicting accounts of the carrying capacity of different types of area and there is a real danger of 'scientific reductionism' in the Hwange National Park, where there appears to be a blanket policy on culling. In reaching these conclusions, Hwange is being compared to certain other parks, such as Tsavo National Park in Kenya, which are by no means similar. True, both Tsavo and Hwange have a rainfall of 600mm each per year, but there are some crucial differences.

Tsavo's rain comes in two or three tranches. Between each rainy period, although there is high humidity at the time, they experience very dry intervals with extensive evapor-transporation (where moisture is thrown off by plants) and evaporation from the soil, which at Tsavo is shallow and alluvial. Much of the rain is immediately lost as flood water.

By contrast, Hwange's main rainy season lasts from December through to February and there is also occasional rain in October and November. Unlike Tsavo's alluvial soil, Hwange's sand, to which I have already made reference, is between 50 and 100 metres deep and has considerable high water retention qualities where much of the rain is held in the top two metres of sand for long periods before it trickles down to the water table.

It does not necessarily follow that because Tsavo is estimated to have a carrying capacity of 13,000 elephants, primarily based on its rainfall of 600 mm, that Hwange's should be the same. If Hwange can support twice as many elephants, (that is the present 26,500 as against the proposed reduced population of 13,000) could you equally back-calculate

that our effective rainfall should be twice that of Tsavo's? How do we know that Hwange, with its diverse vegetation, is not able to support an elephant population twice or three times what we have today?

The extent of the plant biomass at Hwange, has never been measured, yet the main argument given for culling is that the plants are being impacted. In our root systems in the Kalahari woodland area, we learn that 80% of the plant biomass is underground. What effect does this information have on estimates of the elephant carrying capacity at Hwange? No one knows.

Fire

In any ecological management policy, managers must also give sufficient attention to the effects of other phenomena such as frost and fire on the local ecosystem. For example, in 1974, some picnickers caused the fiercest forest fire we have ever had on the Estate while I have been there. It could not be controlled and, such was its intensity, it swept through the entire estate, across many main roads and the railway line and well into the Hwange National Park. The fire followed some years of severe frost and poor rainy seasons, so that there was an immense amount of tinder available. Stands of *Acacia flekii* and Terminalia and other trees were burnt to the ground. Although it took some years to recover, it re-grew more abundantly than ever before. Today the canopy is higher than I ever recall, while the *Acacia flekii* is now three or four metres high in places.

Frost

The keen frost we experience in our part of Zimbabwe 1,000 metres above sea level can have as equally dramatic an effect as fire. Recently we have had seasons of fairly good rainfall and very little frost. The vegetation now is much thicker than it was before the fire, despite an increase in the elephant population.

There can be no doubt that in the normal course of events, we shall again experience heavy frost, which can kill off much of the woody vegetation. Dry years may follow, and again we could be vulnerable to another devastating fire. Yet, as we have experienced on the most recent occasion, fire almost always brings in its aftermath the compensating effect of a substantial increase in vegetation. This may again blanket the area and again thus protect it from the effects of frost. It is a continuous cycle of drought, frost, fire and good rainy seasons. Our ecosystem has adapted itself well to fire and frost because most of it is below ground.

Scientists sometimes refer to fire as a 'total herbivory' since it removes every leaf and may cook the plant and even kill it. Animal herbivory, on the other hand, consists of the removal of leaves and generally need not have much of an impact.

The Elephant: Supreme Landscape Architect

Many people are not fully aware of the positive contribution which elephants make to their (and our) environment.

The underlying Kalahari sands are decomposed sandstone and red in nature so that the further west you go into the desert areas of the south west African coast you will see red sand dunes. Today the topsoil in the Hwange area has evolved into a light grey colour. It is a salutary thought, that in a 10,000 year time-scale, only a metre or so of humus or litter has accumulated above the red layer. It emphasises just how slow the process is that builds up our topsoils in this part of the world.

Throughout the forest, dung beetle's nests are to be found where elephants have defecated. This partnership between these two remarkable creatures is part of the on-going cycle in the maintenance of the habitat in which they and a myriad of other animals, birds and insects live.

Every day, elephants eat approximately 6% of their body weight. In a large animal this can be as much as 200 kgs, or more, of vegetation. They defecate about 16 times a day, producing up to 50 kgs of dung.

The broadest range of Dung Beetles can be found on elephant dung. One type delves straight down, while another draws the dung ball to the stem of a plant to dig it in and plant it by the roots. During the rainy season, when all the dung beetles are about, the dung hardly lasts half a day on the surface. It is removed and taken straight down into ground. The dung beetles actually speed up the whole process of nutrient cycling, providing an energy flow through the system. Thus the elephant eats tons of vegetation, which with the aid of the dung beetle, is returned to the soil in concentrated form. The dung beetle achieves this not only by taking fresh dung into the earth, but he also refines it further by consuming it, making its nutrients more easily utilisable by the plant.

The dung beetles also lay their eggs in the dung. In the process of decomposition, the dung supplies the heat which incubates the eggs. The beetles have to go deep to protect their larvae from being eaten by predators and, when they emerge, the larvae have an ample food supply on which to feed. Inevitably seeds from various plants are inadvertently taken

A bull elephant enjoys a mud bath. Elephants play a key role in habitat modification

Dung beetles roll the balls of soil-encrusted dung to nest sites by pushing them backwards with their hind legs or by strategically balancing on top and propelling them forward

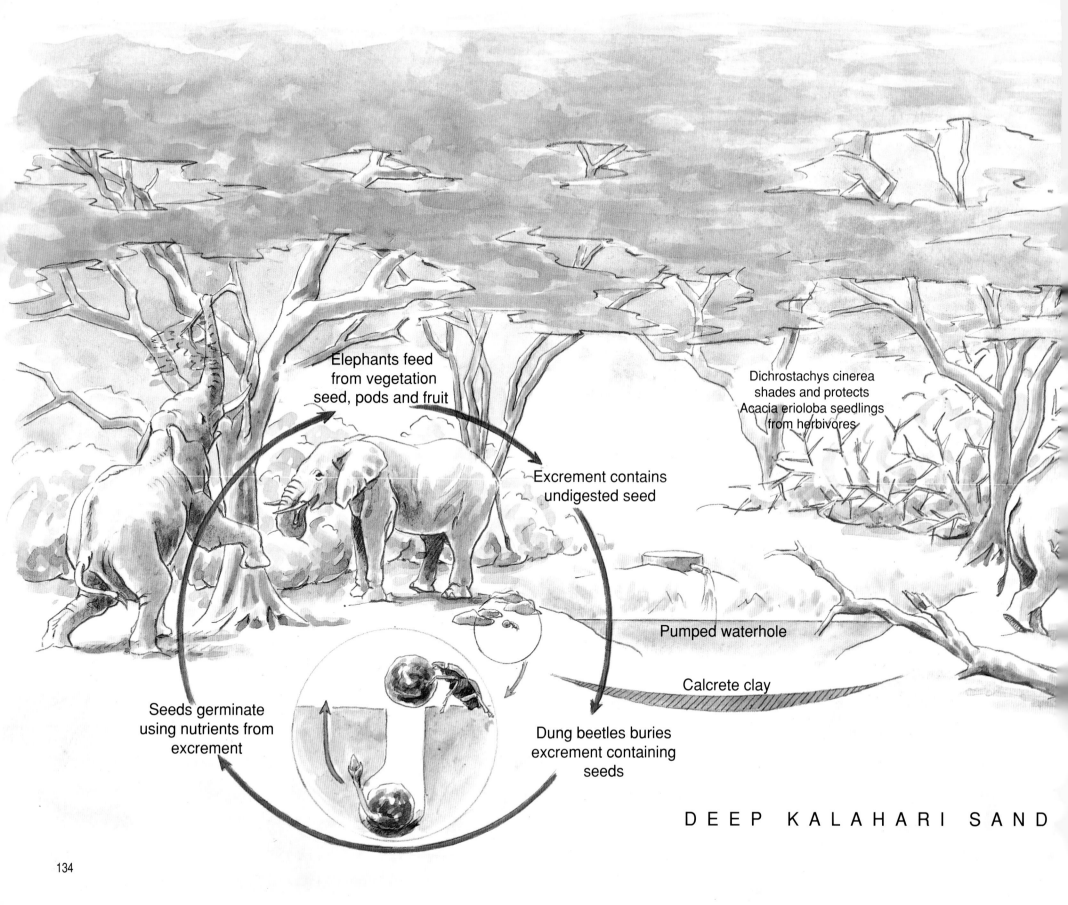

Elephants feed
from vegetation
seed, pods and fruit

Excrement contains
undigested seed

Dichrostachys cinerea
shades and protects
Acacia erioloba seedlings
from herbivores

Pumped waterhole

Calcrete clay

Seeds germinate
using nutrients from
excrement

Dung beetles buries
excrement containing
seeds

DEEP KALAHARI SAND

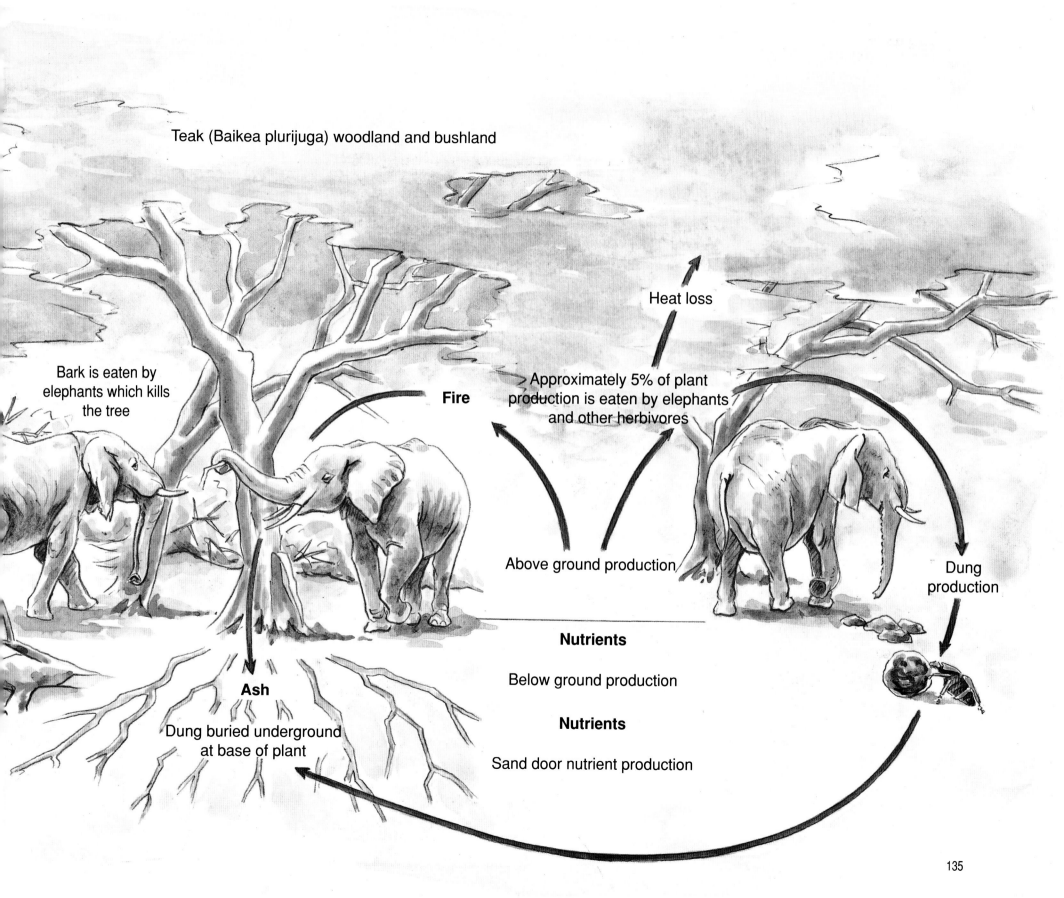

Teak (Baikea plurijuga) woodland and bushland

Heat loss

Bark is eaten by elephants which kills the tree

Fire

Approximately 5% of plant production is eaten by elephants and other herbivores

Above ground production

Dung production

Nutrients

Ash

Below ground production

Dung buried underground at base of plant

Nutrients

Sand door nutrient production

An elephant bull reaches up for a spray of teak leaves, not a favourite food.

Below right: Elephants feed over a wide area. They are able to gather food over five metres above the ground or dig up roots below the surface.

might become moribund.

Interestingly enough, our valuable hardwoods such as the Zimbabwe teaks are hardly touched by elephants, so the important commercial woodland is not at risk. This tree is one of the glories of our forest and provides essential overhead insulating cover against heat and frost, allowing other plants and animals to grow and create an infrastructure under its branches as well as providing shade for elephants and game. The Teak grows to a height of 15 metres or more. It has a large girth, and the wood is very hard. It is much in demand for hard wearing applications such as parquet blocks. A slow growing Zimbabwe Teak will take about 600 years to reach full maturity and 160 years to grow a 350mm girth at chest height. What is extraordinary is that it grows at all in this Kalahari veldt, which largely consists of sand. As I have already mentioned, every particle of sand has been blown in from hundreds of miles away and, in places, it is over 50 metres deep. Equally astonishing is that as much as 80% of the biomass of these big trees is under the ground in huge root systems.

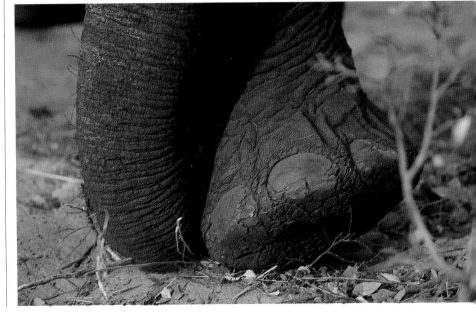

down into the soil, which becomes an ideally fertile base from which to develop.

The feeding habits of elephants have a significant effect in the overall ecology. Many of the trees in the forest will, in some way or other, have been modified by an elephant. This utilisation of the trees by elephants is vital both for the animals and the plants. Without the stimulus for coppicing, which encourages the vigorous growth of next years' shoots, the tree

Sometimes in the forest you can see where the elephants have been excavating for roots with their feet. When they do this, they make hollows in the ground. The Ndebele people talk about 'Mbolisamhlanga', the misty rain that follows the high winds of September and rots the millet stalks in their fields. Knowing about it from my childhood, I believe 'Mbolisamhlanga' has an important function too, here in the Kalahari woodland, when elephants pull leaves off branches and drop them as litter. Some will be blown against the base of the trees and fill up the holes made by elephants and be composted into the ground, thus nourishing root systems on which the elephant had earlier fed.

People talk about destruction when an elephant knocks a tree over, but its effect is to assist growth because the fallen branch provides some measure of protection, while new seeds and grasses germinate and sprout. This is not damage, but elephant utilisation. As far as I am aware, on the Hwange Estate we have the highest density of elephants in the whole of Zimbabwe, with the most animals per square kilometre on a relatively small piece of land. This has not led to devastation but to balanced habitat utilisation. All our mammals are doing well, the vegetation is robust and as it appears at present, can easily continue to support our expanding elephant population for the foreseeable future. This is not to say that we will not be constantly monitoring the situation.

There is no doubt that these proficient animals beneficially affect our, and their, environment. Elephants are supreme gardeners. Just as we go to great lengths to cultivate our gardens, so do elephants in their way, match, virtually everything we do in our gardens. We prune our roses and cultivate around them. We make and apply compost. The elephants are doing the same.

The Megaherbivore Theory

Great efforts are being made by many governments, wildlife agencies and others throughout the world to rescue species in danger and there are conspicuous successes. At the moment, although Loxodonta Africana, the African elephant, is by no means in danger of extinction, the loss of so many of these animals in Africa over the last ten years has set alarm bells ringing. Could it be that the elephant has survived for so many millions of years because he is a dominant force in the shaping of the environment? If so what would happen if he were no longer with us?

Twelve thousand years ago, there were at least 12 types of elephant. After the last Ice Age, there was a mass extinction of megaherbivores in North America. One of the theories is that man over-hunted the very largest mammoths and rhinoceros species that lived there. We know that their numbers were reduced to such a level that either an epidemic or something else killed them all off and there was no longer a viable breeding stock.

This was followed by a mass extinction of many of the smaller herbivores, which were also hunted by man because they were big, easy to find and provided quantities of meat. The extinction of the megaherbivores it is thought adversely affected a whole train of other herbivores, because those very large, and presumably intelligent animals, like our elephants today, created in that far off time, an 'environment of patchiness'. That is, where there might once have been extensive woodlands, the elephants and the mammoths would go and devastate an area. This would become a patchwork of different environments - woodland here, a bushland there, open and closed areas, where previously there had been just one. These new habitats created new niches for all other animals to live. When they were eliminated, the environment returned to its original homogeneity. All those that relied on the patchy

Elephants enjoy
playing in water and
are also good
swimmers.

habitat were unable to survive because the elephants or mammoths were not there any more.

The New Ecological Thinking

The new ecological thinking in Zimbabwe's National Parks, with which I have considerable empathy, is to preserve heterogeneity, but not merely for a few favoured animals or plants. The desire is to preserve everything. That raises some serious questions. Man, by reducing these 'natural' areas. has created substantial 'edge effects' on National Parks, creating little islands which are not necessarily self-sustaining. What therefore should be done inside the Parks to try and keep them as heterogeneous as possible? No one would want a park filled with a million elephants. There would not be room for anything else, but what is the answer?

Alternate Population Control

I have always suggested that elephants themselves were capable of an element of natural birth control, and I believe we should be prepared to undertake research, if necessary, in enforced homeo-stasis. Without intervention, in hard times of food scarcity, cows have come into season less regularly and males have not been so eager to mate. At periods of violent population reduction in any species the birthrate rises.

Elephants have always had the capacity to self regulate their numbers. In the past, if they were exterminated in one area and there was a breeding stock in another, they would eventually recolonise. Now man has impacted the world so much, that even if elephants were sufficiently reduced, it is not inconceivable that the species might fall below the genetic safety level, with nowhere else for the gene pool to be re-established. This is a somewhat far-fetched and apocalyptic prospect, but many game reserves in Africa have already become islands and it is there the argument about culling is

most vigorous, and it is claimed, with some justification, that we no longer have a natural ecosystem and man has to think about looking after our whole environment like a little park.

Co-operation

Since the inception of our sanctuary, we have lost numerous elephants. Some of our best known bulls have been shot for encroaching on the airstrip, others for raiding gardens in suburban Dete, whilst others have been mistaken for Park bulls and shot as part of a population reduction exercise. Hwange Estate is bounded to a large extent by land under the control of the Forestry Commission, some of this land is on lease for game-viewing activities, whilst the rest is utilised by the Commission for hunting safaris. Should any of the authorities wish to eliminate a large number of elephants, for example, for "scientific" reasons, they could do so and we would be powerless to intervene. In recent years we have experienced increasing co-operation and understanding from all of the officials with whom we share common boundaries. Nevertheless, situations can change and so can people. We have come to appreciate more and more the necessity for guaranteed long-term protection for what are now the Presidential Elephants.

It is an almost instinctive reaction of wildlife managers in Zimbabwe to conclude that if "culling" is not immediately necessary, then at some time in the future it will become necessary.

I question the validity of a blanket approach to culling in an area as large and ecologically diverse as the Park. If the fragile areas to the north are perceived to be in danger of becoming permanently damaged, then those areas should be managed accordingly. The areas of Kalahari woodland in the south should then be viewed separately. Perhaps the greatest danger to our elephant population is that the scientists, who sincerely

A bull elephant gently caresses a receptive female in a display of affection.

believe that culling is the safe option, have no opportunity to put their theories to the test. One of the most effective methods of measuring the effects of culling is to compare it with a similar and adjacent area where there is no culling. The ecological assumptions can then be put to the test. Hwange Estate, where there is no culling, could be an ideal testing ground. One potentially fruitful area of research into population control with the herd, might be the testing of various methods of contraception, an option we infinitely prefer to killing. The scope for controlled research is considerable and offers outstanding opportunities for our scientists to work with the Presidential Elephants. It is our hope that in an atmosphere of enthusiasm and candour, a meaningful cross-flow of information will take place between scientists working in the National Park and on Hwange Estate.

How Many Elephants is Too Many?

Already some people are questioning what we will do when we get too many elephants. I do not know what "too many" elephants is. What some people call "degradation" I honestly call "utilisation". At the present-time we have observed a rapid increase in elephant numbers. Our population is getting older, with minimal natural mortality. When the rate of natural increment slows down or when natural mortality increases amongst old animals and calves, it could be an indication that the elephants have reached something approaching optimum density. High-powered scientists may brand me naive, emotional or downright irresponsible, but deep down, I have great faith in ecological processes to provide the solutions. Everything takes time, and speedy intervention or over-management by us could trigger unknown catastrophes in the future.

In 1974, I estimated that there were 22 elephants in the sanctuary and a small number of itinerant bulls. Now, at the end of 1991, there are more than 300 animals. Obviously the increase has not been totally due to births, although many calves have been born over the past 16 years. A number of elephants have moved into the area. Every now and again a totally new animal moves in and is immediately noticed because of a special physical characteristic.

Just recently, we have had Carrot, a young bull with an abnormally large tusk shaped like a carrot seemingly wedged into his mouth. An interesting visit lasting two months was made by a large cow with a floppy ear. She became known as Disc and is most certainly a cow of high rank from one of the cow herds resident in Hwange National Park. Both of these animals have again moved away but obviously many others, particularly young bulls, have taken up permanent residence. Immigrants are usually noticeable by their initial timidity, but soon gain confidence from the relaxed behaviour of the others.

Ambassadors of Goodwill

Today, game viewing is flourishing on Hwange Estate with vehicles from the Hwange Safari Lodge, Sikumi Tree Lodge and Sable Valley Lodge departing on safaris daily. There is a rich diversity of wildlife which is easily approached. However, it is the amenable elephants which create the greatest excitement for foreign visitors. We have built on the initial cautious acceptance of Tatty Ear and her family and it is now possible to sit in the middle of a milling group of over one hundred unconcerned elephants.

We have been living amongst a population of elephants that increasingly becomes more and more adapted to the presence of humans in the shape of tourists. Due to the quality of the experience, visitors to Zimbabwe feel a special affinity towards the individual elephants they encounter on their safari.

The elephants themselves have become our ambassadors of goodwill, as well as a powerful marketing tool for our tourist trade. In effect, the elephants daily prove their worth in economic terms.

Some people argue that wildlife must "pay its way". Generally they believe this means killing game, selling the by-products and the pleasure of the hunt. The message sent out by the elephants of the Hwange Estate is that they are worth more to Zimbabwe alive than dead. Despite this, it is folly to measure everything in economic terms. We prefer to take the view that these elephants, apart from their obvious financial benefit to the nation, are worthy of the utmost protection just because they are elephants; because they are part of us and the land we share.

A Parliamentary Visit

The Deputy Minister of Transport, Mrs Amina Hughes, came to the Hwange Estate in 1990 with a delegation of Australian parliamentarians on an official visit to Zimbabwe. I had the great pleasure of taking Mrs Hughes and members of her party on safari.

We drove out from the Hwange Safari Lodge at night onto the Dete vlei. It was pitch black with no moon. I switched off the engine and lights and we sat in complete darkness in the middle of a party of about ten of our friendly bull elephants grazing on the summer grasses. They came up to within a metre of us, magnificent animals each as large as a house.

It was an overwhelming experience for our guests and afterwards Mrs Hughes was kind enough to listen to an idea which had been developing in my mind for some time. I wanted to ensure that for all time, these elephants and their descendents could roam forever free and that their range would not be annihilated by man, and that the ancient forests, the open woodland and grassy valleys would not be levelled in the name of human development.

Could there somehow be a way of *permanently* protecting this gentle herd of elephants, in which the President might wish to be involved? Might he even consider the possibility of putting our

elephant herd under the protection of the Presidential Office as a symbol of Zimbabwe's well-known commitment to responsible wild life management? A precedent had been set with the mighty Ahmed, at that time the largest of Kenya's living elephants. President Kenyatta issued a Presidential Decree bestowing immunity from hunting or poaching on that world-famous animal. Ahmed lived out his natural life. This was the inspiration.

I was asking for special recognition for a whole herd of elephants by the Head of State, something which had never been done before anywhere else in the world. I believe Mrs Hughes had greatly enjoyed the close contact with the animals, but more importantly, she also immediately appreciated the potential value of this particular herd of special elephants both for Zimbabwe's growing tourist industry and as a practical demonstration in what could be achieved in wildlife conservation. She enthusiastically promised to discuss the matter with her colleagues in the Government.

Presidential Status

Comrade Didymus Mutasa, the Senior Minister for Political Affairs, who has taken a great interest in what we have been doing on the Hwange Estate, personally undertook to present the whole matter personally to the President. To my great joy, His Excellency President Robert Mugabe agreed to give his official patronage to the Hwange Estate elephants. Upon his assent, they have become *'The Presidential Elephants of Zimbabwe.'*

Research Trust

To justify the President's confidence, we are in the process of setting up a Zimbabwe elephant research trust, the principal objectives of which will be to sponsor and support a wide range of elephant field research projects in our part of the world and encourage the young Zimbabwean graduate scientists of tomorrow to become involved with our work. I, personally, am also looking forward to obtaining approval to welcome, amongst others, international experts in genetics and infrasound communication. The work will need to be funded and it is encouraging that we have already been approached with offers of substantial help by several international research funding organisations. At the same time it is incumbent on us to ensure that the area does not become spoiled, but retains its wild beauty. Should it ever become 'over-commercialised' in a western sense, then the magic will be lost for ever. I anticipate our new trust taking on board the important responsibility of acting as our conscience, so that the integrity of our efforts may be maintained.

An Assured Future

There is no doubt that the Presidential Elephants of Zimbabwe will become as world famous as the gorillas of Zaire and Uganda or the tigers of India. Their high status will stimulate tourist revenues. More and more people will want to come and see them and they will become a key focal point for vital research funding. In the foreseeable future, I envisage the Presidential Elephants of Zimbabwe expanding in numbers and extending their range into adjoining forestry areas and private game ranches. When this happens, local people will benefit from the increased revenue to be earned from tourists eager to see these friendly and famous animals. Non-hunting safari camps will spring up. Safari operators and ranchers will view the elephants as "their" elephants. Perhaps they will learn to love them as deeply as I do. And perhaps the days of slaughter, pursuit and harassment will be over for them and their offspring forever.

Thanks to President Robert Mugabe, the Presidential Elephants of Zimbabwe will never again have to justify their existence with their blood and ivory.